PREPARING FOR SERVICE

A History of Higher Education in the Church of God

by
Barry L. Callen

WARNER PRESS, INC.
Anderson, IN

Published by
Warner Press, Inc.
Anderson, Indiana

All scripture passages, unless otherwise indicated, are from the King James Version © 1972 by Thomas Nelson or the Revised Standard Version © 1972 by Thomas Nelson.

Copyright © 1988 by Warner Press, Inc.
ISBN 0-87162-586-5 Stock # D6225
All Rights Reserved
Printed in the United States of America
Warner Press, Inc.

Arlo F. Newell, Editor-in-Chief
Dan Harman, Book Editor

Table of Contents

	Page
Acknowledgment	v
Introduction	vi
List of Tables	ix

Chapters:

    I. **The Troubled Setting** 1
        The American Tradition
        Challenges to Faith
        A Reformation Movement Emerges

    II. **Education Without Colleges** 12
        Beware of Formal Education!
        The Sunday School
        The Missionary Homes
        A Crucial Year—1917

    III. **The Story of Anderson University**
        (College and School of Theology) 25

    IV. **The Story of Arlington College**
        (Azusa Pacific University) 51

    V. **The Story of Bay Ridge Christian College** 65

    VI. **The Story of Gardner Bible College** 78

    VII. **The Story of Mid-America Bible College** 90

    VIII. **The Story of Warner Memorial University** 103

    IX. **The Story of Warner Pacific College** 111

    X. **The Story of Warner Southern College** 126

    XI. **The Story of West Indies Theological College** 140

**XII. Responsible Relationship Between
      Church and Colleges** 154
      Some Beginning Guidelines
      Steps Toward a Permanent Commission
      Exploration and Frustration
      Final Step to Permanence
      Work of the Commission
      To Facilitate or Control?
      A New Beginning
      Looking Back for Perspective
XIII. General Observations and Concerns 185
Appendix A: Criteria for Establishing New Colleges 196
**Appendix B: Who's Who in Church of God
               Higher Education** 200
**Appendix C: International Institutions
               Related to the Church of God** 214
Index of Persons 216

Acknowledgment

An undertaking of this magnitude could not have been completed without the cooperation of many persons. Dozens have shared from their personal records and memories. The current presidents of the institutions have read carefully the chapters on their respective campuses to help insure proper perspective and accuracy of detail. The editor-in-chief of Warner Press has been a constant encouragement during the several years of research and writing.

I express my gratitude to all who shared with me in this review of the past and this look to the future. To work with the histories of these institutions is to come to love them and to be deeply grateful for the vision of their founders.

Barry L. Callen
Anderson, Indiana
June, 1988

Introduction

From the very beginning of the Church of God movement in the final quarter of the nineteenth century there was a sense of divine vision and urgency among its people. They wanted to do the will of God for their times. Many felt the evening time of the gospel age was at hand and a bright new day was dawning. Time was short, workers were few, and it was so important to get out the news!

The result? There was a boldness among them; there was also a humbleness. They believed that God would give freely of his grace and the many special gifts necessary for the expansion and nuturing of his true church. This gave motivation and confidence. But these excited disciples were well aware of their own limitations in the face of human frailties and the immensity of the task. Thus they also were humble and desired to prepare for their service in the best way possible.

This present volume is the story of their journey to discover the most appropriate and effective ways to become better prepared to fulfill their high calling from God. In particular, it recalls the issues, attitudes, experiments, and institutions of higher education that emerged along the way.

While eventually this movement of the Church of God became worldwide and developed various educational programs in many countries, the following study is limited to a consideration of events and institutions in the United States, Canada, and the West Indies. It is further limited to institutions which continue to exist today, except for Arlington College (which continues in another form) and Warner Memorial University. Other educational programs such as Berean Bible College, Gordon Bible School, Kansas City Bible Training School, and Southern Bible Institute, have

been excluded from extended consideration because of their relatively brief existence and/or the restricted scope of their programs.
God calls all of his children to serve. Institutions of higher education have become a major means by which the Church of God has sought to assist persons to prepare for that service. Higher education has attracted much attention and required many dollars. The colleges and seminary have become very influential in the life of the church, and sometimes controversial. They have been significant cohesive forces, as well as centers of activity, creativity, and relationship building. They have helped a loosely organized church fellowship to focus its identity, extend its borders, and both conserve and rethink its history, teaching, and traditions. Their story must be known if the history of the Church of God movement itself is ever to be understood.

Higher education in the Church of God has come to rest in part on a conviction which was stated this way in the 1920-1921 catalog of Anderson Bible Training School (now Anderson University): "Though many have seemed to decrease in spirituality while increasing in knowledge, the reverse should be the case—better qualified men should be more spiritual men."

But informed spirituality has not been the only goal in the church's higher education. Personal maturity and professional preparation and effectiveness also have been essential concerns over the years. So has the need to be free and able to think for oneself in the service of God, the church, and humankind.

Two outstanding men have embodied well the addressing of this latter goal during the formative decades of higher education of the Church of God. One, Russell R. Byrum, has been described by Robert H. Reardon as the man who "threw open the windows and doors of learning." He was a teacher-scholar who "encouraged his students to explore frontiers and to drink at the great fountain of historic thought." According to Reardon, "It was largely through the breadth and vision of this man that we were saved as a movement from theological rigidity and the same kind of closed-mindedness our movement had come into being to oppose."[1]

The other, Otto F. Linn, was one of those people who has been, in the words of church historian Merle D. Strege, "captured by our notion that the truth may be pursued more than possessed. He firmly opposed authoritarian control of some minds by other minds." Linn, Byrum, and many other educational pioneers who appear in the following pages "sounded a note of scholarship and insisted with quiet determination that we begin to read and understand the Bible in light of that scholarship. They introduced us to the realm of learning."[2] It was seen as an indispensable part of the needed preparation for service from which thousands upon thousands now have benefited. It is quite a story!

Notes
[1] *Vital Christianity,* May 4, 1980, p. 5.
[2] *Vital Christianity,* December 7, 1986, pp. 18-19.

List of Tables

Table   **Page**

1. Overview of the Founding of Ten Institutions 23
2. Anderson University: Leaders, Accreditations 47
3. Anderson University, School of Theology: Sources of New Seminarians 49
4. Arlington College (Azusa Pacific University): Leaders, Accreditations 63
5. Bay Ridge Christian College: Leaders, Accreditations 76
6. Gardner Bible College: Leaders, Accreditations 88
7. Mid-America Bible College: Leaders, Accreditations 101
8. Warner Memorial University: Leaders, Accreditations .. 108
9. Warner Pacific College: Leaders, Accreditations 124
10. Warner Southern College: Leaders, Accreditations 138
11. West Indies Theological College: Leaders, Accreditations 153
12. Officers, Commission on Christian Higher Education ... 175
13. Central Agenda Items, Commission on Christian Higher Education 176
14. Enrollment Study: 1966-1987 179
15. First-time Church of God Freshmen: 1970-1987 180
16. Graduates by Degree: 1981-1987 182
17. Church Support for Higher Education 183
18. World Service Dollars Per FTE Student 184

Chapter 1
The Troubled Setting

The colleges associated with the Church of God (Anderson, Indiana) are the inheritors of a long tradition of higher education in the United States. Knowing at least the highlights and trends of that tradition is essential to understanding what has developed within the Church of God and why it had such difficulty even getting started.

The American Tradition

As early as 1619, when 10,000 acres of land were granted by the Virginia Company for America's first university, the goal was to combine classical learning and the Christian religion for the sake of cultivating "the humane person." Clearly in the tradition of England's seventeenth-century colleges at Oxford and Cambridge and the Scottish universities, this new school sought to provide a general education which emphasized the arts of clear thinking and effective communication and the principles which ought to direct all personal and public affairs. Unfortunately, malaria and an Indian massacre ended this initial venture by 1622.

Very soon, however, learning and religion joined forces again. This time it was the Puritans. They established Harvard College in 1636, patterning it after Emmanuel College of Cambridge University in England. This new school became the first of a series of colonial institutions which lifted high the banner of Christ in the context of serious academic study. The central purpose of these new schools was represented well by Harvard's famous statement of beginning:

> After God had carried us safe to New England, and we had builded our houses, provided necessaries for our livelihood, rear'd convenient places for God's worship, and settled the Civil Government: One of the next things we longed for, and looked after was to advance Learning, and perpetuate it to Posterity, dreading to leave an illiterate ministry to the churches, when our present Ministers shall lie in the Dust.[1]

The charter of William and Mary, the next American college, declared that it was to exist so that "the church of Virginia may be furnished with a seminary for Ministers of the Gospel, and that the youth may be piously educated in good letters and manners, and that the Christian faith may be propagated amongst the Western Indians to the glory of Almighty God." And the next, Yale, was founded in 1701 by a group of ministers as a school "wherein youth may be instructed in the arts & sciences, who through the blessing of Almighty God may be fitted for public employment, both in church and civil state."[2]

In general, collegiate training in America found its parent and main sponsor in the Christian churches. Religion was unashamedly recognized as the keystone of the educational arch. The Christian faith in particular was the determining factor in educational theory and practice. This is exactly how most Americans wanted it and how it had been for centuries before the birth of Harvard. The God of the Christian was recognized as the ground of truth and, therefore, the guiding light and ruling principle in the education of the young.

Such a central place for the Christian faith was really a continuance of the medieval university tradition in a New World setting. The medieval mind had tended to conceive the whole of human society as unified in Christ through his royal, priestly, and prophetic roles. These roles were understood to be embodied in the three major earthly institutions, namely the state, based on law; the church, founded on revelation, and the university, upheld by reason. Even today the relatedness of these institutions is preserved by the symbolism of the gowns worn by the justices in court, the ministers in church, and the professors and graduates in college commencements.

This European heritage of higher learning did not perish in the American wilderness as many assumed it would. Its beginnings in the New World may have been fragile, more promise than performance at first, and certainly affected by the practical needs and limitations of a young nation. But higher learning was planted securely on American shores and it did survive.

The nature of this higher learning was more deeply concerned with forming character than with fostering pure academic research. It placed great value on a controlled residential pattern of life for students. It oriented itself primarily toward the training of a special elite for community leadership. Early American higher education was intended to educate gentlemen and professionals. At first it concentrated on preparing ministers, but soon lawyers, doctors, and teachers were included. Hebrew, Greek, Latin, and classical history and literature were basic to the curriculum. And the whole frame of reference for this curriculum was dominated by the assumptions and goals of the Christian faith.

During the nineteenth century Americans tended to group themselves by occupation, social class, religion, sex, locality, and ethnic background. Almost all of these groups found adequate reason to set up their own colleges, both to perpetuate their own subcultures and to give themselves legitimacy in larger society. Hundreds of colleges owed their entire existence to the vision and energy of a single person.

The numerous Christian denominations in the United States, themselves significant subcultures, provided a tremendous impulse for college founding. They were motivated by the need for an educated ministry and by a missionary spirit which sought to establish new and vital centers of Christian education and living. They also were motivated by the concerns of strengthening denominational loyalty, competing with denominational rivals, and off-setting the "secularistic" influences spreading throughout the culture.

Particularly after 1819, when the Supreme Court's decision in the Dartmouth College case essentially assured private institutions freedom from state interference, private liberal arts colleges multiplied. By 1860 over five hundred new colleges had been founded, most of them under church sponsorship. Though many of these did not survive the Civil War years (particularly those in the South) and though they were very weak institutions by modern standards, the American historians Samuel Eliot Morison and Henry Steele Commager have praised a strength they surely did have:

> For an integrated education, one that cultivates manliness and makes gentlemen as well as scholars, one that disciplines the social affections and trains young men to faith in God, consideration for his fellow men, and respect for learning, America has never had the equal of her hill-top colleges.[3]

And so it remained in the United States without significant change for many generations. Faith and learning went hand-in-hand. Together they were an essential part of the backbone of a young nation.

Almost from the beginning, however, there were contrary forces. Changes of major proportions came along. These changes caused many Christian people to distrust higher education and even to fear that cultivation of the mind might be dangerous to the life of faith and a direct threat to the health of the church.

Challenges to Faith

The claims of the Christian faith may indeed have enjoyed great prestige and have influenced the basic nature of higher education in America from the beginning. But all of this came to face decades of change and turmoil. Traditional piety began to be pitched out many windows. Theological and political assumptions, virtually unquestioned for centuries, came under attack—and much of the action inevitably came to focus on college campuses.

By the end of the eighteenth century the dominant beliefs and values of the early colonial period were being challenged directly. Critical crosscurrents were blowing vigorously in some quarters. Orthodox Christianity was beginning to struggle to hold its own against philosophies of the "Enlightenment" which were taking hold in some intellectual circles. New approaches and names filled the air, approaches like rationalism, deism, naturalism, and empiricism and names like Descartes, Bacon, Hobbes, Locke, and Rousseau.[4] In America the bitter writings of Thomas Paine and the milder ones of Thomas Jefferson tended to encourage a style of religious unbelief typical of the European skeptics and political radicals of the time. From a Christian perspective, therefore, by the latter part of the eighteenth century there was a general decline in the American public's commitment to traditional religion and morals. Timothy Dwight, who became president of Yale in 1795, described increasing numbers of college students of the day:

> Youths . . . with strong passions and feeble principles . . . delighted in the prospect of unrestrained gratification . . . and became enamored with the new doctrines. . . . Striplings scarcely fledged suddenly found that the world had been enveloped in general darkness through the long succession of preceding ages, and that the light of human wisdom had just begun to dawn upon the human race.[5]

An anti-church play was staged at Dartmouth. When the dean of Princeton opened the chapel Bible to read, a pack of playing cards fell out. Someone had carved a rectangle out of each page to accommodate the pack—and to infuriate the school!

In the decades that followed there were times of dramatic spiritual awakening on the nation's campuses that brought back some of the mutual supportiveness between learning and religion. But society-wide trends were pointed the other way. Interest in the natural sciences was rising. Pressure was increasing for higher education to be freed from the control of religious bodies. It was argued that the mind of man must be unfettered, loosed to reason boldly and act even revolutionarily on behalf of human happiness. The industrial progress of the nation was developing a need for persons with specialized training not available in the usual liberal arts curriculum that characterized most church-related colleges.

With the emergence of a more open society during the early decades of the nineteenth century, the inherited educational system began to be challenged. The historian Richard Hofstadter concludes: "American society was too democratic to accept completely the idea of a gentleman's education, too practical . . . to continue to accept complacently its classical content, too dynamic and competitive to accept indefinitely its static character."[6]

Something very new was bound to come along. That something would be more "secular" and practical, more "scientific" and specifically related to the materialistic needs and desires of a changing society. No longer would higher education be designed to get as much as possible of the body of Christian truth into the heads of undergraduates under the assumption that there is a more or less fixed body of truth. Rather, it would view knowledge more as a progressive field of inquiry freed from religious presuppositions and restrictions.

In 1862 the Congress of the United Stated passed and President Lincoln signed the Morrill Act endowing new colleges of agriculture and mechanical arts in many states. These land-grant colleges broke radically with the historic pattern of liberal education (the Ivy League classical ideal) by emphasizing the "practical" branches of knowledge so necessary for an expanding young nation. They also separated their educational work from church control. Cornell University, founded in 1865, was the earliest example of a frankly secular university established to meet the needs of an emerging industrial society. Its charter stated clearly that "persons of every religious denomination or of no religious denomination shall be equally eligible to all offices and appointments." It was to be a new day. It was a day which saw the money to finance a rapidly expanding academic community coming not from Christian bodies, which had been the financial foundation of the past, but from the federal government and industrialists.

Another development equally abhorred by most church-related educators of the day was the importation of the German university model of higher education, something dramatized by the founding of Johns Hopkins University in 1876. Defenders of traditional church-related colleges spared little in denouncing this major development. John Blanchard wrote in 1892: "German universities have done more to make the Bible contemptible than have all other causes since Luther rescued it from the convent of Erfort."[7]

Between 1815 and World War I more than ten thousand American students journeyed to Germany to secure their Ph.D. degrees from prestigious universities like Heidelberg, Leipzig, and Berlin. In those settings they learned a new model of education and picked up viewpoints about the Christian faith that were considered heretical at home. The new model gave priority to studies at the doctoral level, stressed faculty research and degraded undergraduate education (the typical college years) to little more than preparation for postgraduate specialization. Heavy emphasis was placed on freedom—freedom for students to elect their own courses of study and for faculty members to teach subjects of their choice and to pursue sophisticated research.

Here was a far more scientific, technical, and specialized notion of scholarship. The spirit of critical inquiry into any subject was fostered. Nothing, including the Bible, was to be immune from the severest of investigation. No longer was there to be any orthodoxy except belief in the right to pursue truth in a setting freed from artificial restraints on the scholarly process. Emphasis was usually placed on factual knowledge rather than on meaning and morals. The prime goal was the acquiring of relevant data and not the nurturing of persons. These were a few of the key building blocks for what later would be a network of state universities in which most American youth would be educated.

The methods of this German model of higher education were soon directed at the pages of the Bible. What resulted was a stress on the "human" side of sacred literature wherein, presumably, one could discover the cultural shaping and historical errors that comprised such revered pages. Professors became bold as they passed their independent judgments on the questionable validity of various parts of the Bible. The result? There were several.

German universities became world famous for producing creative scholars in many fields of professional endeavor. Material prosperity did come from some of the new knowledge gained from such an approach. But this general approach to higher education, whether carried on in Germany or by its many American imitators, became infamous in the eyes of much of the nineteenth-century Christian community. Beyond the fact that challenges to accepted Christian doctrine were upsetting, it became especially objectionable when such "enlightened" persons joined the faculties of church-related colleges. In some institutions the educational process deteriorated into bitter battles for control. In others the new trends were decried and every attempt was made to continue business as usual in isolation from such unwelcome developments.

Reaction to the encroachment of this "modernism" was so severe in some quarters that many traditional and especially church-related colleges found themselves alienated from the culture around them. The historian of Wheaton College in Illinois, for instance, reported: "As the waves of 'modern thought' swept over America, Wheaton College gradually became an island of resistance in a turbulent sea of doubt."[8] Renewed concern for heartfelt religion swelled and joined with a disgust for this wave of unbelief to lead many orthodox Christian believers to a mistrust of human reason itself. The reaction often was one of anger and shock and a pulling away from what was judged to be the increasingly corrupted scene of higher education.

Social and educational trends were multiplying against the church-related college and were saying that such colleges were relics of the past. By 1900 many persons had concluded that the small Christian college was living on borrowed time. William Rainey Harper surveyed prospects for numerous denominational colleges scattered across the Midwest and judged that only 25 percent of them had a good chance for survival. The rest would either scale down their programs or die.[9] The trend away from a narrow sectarian spirit in religion coupled with the growing strength and vocational versatility of the state-supported institutions all suggested difficulty if not doom for the small church college which championed traditional assumptions and was desperate for dollars.

As the twentieth century was ready to dawn, it was common in evangelical pulpits and holiness camp meetings to hear tirades against formal learning, almost as if such learning were little more than a cunning wile of the devil designed to draw a person away from dependence on the grace of God. Seminaries were commonly condemned as "cemeteries." Many unlettered spokespersons for "the old-time religion" were given enthusiastic hearings on almost any subject they cared to address. Higher education had fallen under the cloud of a haughty attempt to lean on one's own understanding. Billy Sunday, the most flamboyant of urban revivalists of the early twentieth century, boomed on the subject with a rugged rhetoric:

> Thousands of college graduates are going as fast as they can straight to hell. If I had a million dollars I'd give $999,999 to the church and $1 to education. When the word of God says one thing and scholarship says another, scholarship can go to hell![10]

It often is noted that such negative attitudes toward learning came partly from the social status of the persons involved. For instance, early nineteenth-century Methodism in the United States enlisted its greatest support among the lower classes, especially those living in frontier areas. Because of the rather primitive style of life, these persons rarely had the time, money, energy, or even opportunity to devote to higher learning. As the historian of Taylor University in Indiana concluded:

> What they could not obtain, many of them decried as inherently evil. Thus the Methodists of this period talked much of the dangers of "book learning"—especially about how it made ministers "less spiritual." They often confused being "less spiritual" with being less emotional than the average Methodist in one's approach to religion.[11]

Whatever explanation one chooses, by 1900 conservative Christianity in the United States had reacted dramatically. The resurgence of "holiness" teaching had brought with it a considerable isolation from "the world," including the world of learning. It had led to a lack of interest in art, literature, science, and general culture. Christians by the thousands had retired from the mainstream of society and had placed their faith squarely in the authority of their personal experiences with Christ. While the "modernists" were undercutting the public's traditional confidence in the Bible, many conservative Christians had become rigid in their views, sometimes blindly defending the faith against all comers. Faith and learning were at odds. It was a troubled time.

A Reformation Movement Emerges

The Church of God reformation movement made its first modest appearance on the American scene in the late nineteenth century. By then church-related higher education already had known its day of glory and now was living through a controversial and chaotic period.

This new Christian movement was in strong reaction to the turmoil of rampant denominationalism. The focus of its vision was that:

> the church is the spiritual body of Christ . . . that the denominations are only religious organizations brought about by Christian people and are not in reality churches in the New Testament sense. The ideal was that, if all Christians could . . . abide in Christ alone, that would be the road to oneness in the church.[12]

Feeling strongly that ecclesiastical organizations erode the leadership of the Holy Spirit in the church, these Christians "came out" of all denominational entanglements. They sought to accept the apostolic faith as defined in the New Testament and to fulfill its mission in an open and free fellowship of sanctified and unified believers.

The pioneers of this movement, therefore, were heavily experience-oriented (in common with many conservative Christians of the time) and also were quite anti-institutional in general outlook. They were disgusted with denominational rivalries and were less than impressed with the tendency of denominations to found colleges as part of that competitive process. The emphasis on experience and away from institutions, plus the general tenor of the times, led to considerable caution about the appropriateness of actually establishing "Church of God" institutions for the purpose of fostering the life of the mind. Quite understandably, then, higher education got off to a very slow start in the Church of God.

Notes

[1] *New England's First Fruits.* Old South Leaflets, Vol. III, No. 51 (Boston: Directors of the Old South Work, n.d.), p. 1.

[2] As quoted by Richard Hofstadter and C. DeWitt Hardy, *The Development and Scope of Higher Education in the United States* (New York: Columbia University Press, 1952), p. 4.

[3] Samuel Eliot Morison and Henry Steele Commager, *The Growth of the American Republic* (New York: Oxford University Press, 1950), p. 514.

[4] A review of these intellectual tensions is found in R. F. Butts and L. A. Cremin, *A History of Education in American Culture* (New York: Holt, 1953), pp. 43-63 and Howard Lowry, *The Mind's Adventure* (Philadelphia: The Westminster Press, 1950), pp. 20-33.

[5] Timothy Dwight, as quoted by C. Robert Pace, *Education and Evangelism* (The Carnegie Commission on Higher Education, 1972), p. 10.

[6] Hofstadter and Hardy, *Development and Scope of Higher Education,* p. 22.

[7] John Blanchard in the *Congregational News,* (Chicago, January, 1892).

[8] W. Wyeth Willard, *Fire on the Prairie* (Wheaton, Ill.: Van Kampen Press, 1950), p. 68.
[9] William Rainey Harper, *The Trend in Higher Education* (Chicago: University of Chicago Press, 1905), pp. 349ff.
[10] As quoted by Richard Hofstadter, *Anti-Intellectualism in American Life* (New York: Alfred A. Knopf, 1962), p. 122.
[11] William C. Ringenberg, *Taylor University* (Grand Rapids: Eerdmans, 1973). p. 13.
[12] John A. Morrison, *As the River Flows* (Anderson, IN: Anderson College Press, 1962), p. 165.

Chapter 2
Education Without Colleges

In the earliest decades of the history of the Church of God movement it happened just about the way one would have expected. Given an experience oriented, anti-institutionally minded, generally rural body of Christian people, full of zeal and urgency for a gospel cause, living in the middle of revolutionary changes in American higher education that rarely were friendly to the faith, founding colleges was not a high priority. To the contrary, formal learning and evangelistic believing tended to be seen more as competitors than as companions. Education was identified as a typical part of the sectarian scene that God was calling to an end.

Beware of Formal Education!

Soon after his conversion experience in 1865 Daniel S. Warner attended Oberlin College in Ohio, enrolling for an English preparatory course. There he was exposed to persons of learning and refinement. At the time the president of the college was Charles Finney, the nation's foremost preacher and writer of holiness. Later Warner attended Vermillion College where he studied Greek and New Testament.

In 1876, when Warner was a Winebrennerian minister, the West Ohio Eldership met in Findlay, Ohio, and expressed its belief "that in no other way can we so effectually build up the Church and retain the children of our brotherhood than by establishing an institution of learning to be owned and controlled by the Church."[1] Warner was one of three ministers appointed to plan a way to bring such a thing about (the resulting institution continues to this day as Findlay College).

But the presumed significance of such an educational institution was not high on Warner's agenda in the years that followed, even though he was himself a highly motivated reader, researcher, and writer. As a mature minister later separated from the Winebrennerian brotherhood, starting institutions of any kind (especially ones such as colleges intended in part to solidify denominational loyalty) was seen as far from acceptable. He once wrote in the *Gospel Trumpet* that the only credentials required for ministry were "to be filled with the Holy Spirit and have a reasonable knowledge of the English language." On another occasion he expressed his deep suspicions about much in higher education: "Colleges are necessary to fit men for the work of the devil and the business of the world. . . . They are but devil's playhouses."[2]

A major manuscript of Warner's was revised and completed by H. M. Riggle after Warner's death in 1895. It was an extensive critique of the "sects" based on biblical prophecy. Particularly criticized as a "mark of the Beast" was the denominational practice of instilling particular sectarian doctrines in the minds of their adherents. Warner and Riggle pictured education as a tool to solidify the disastrous disunity of God's church. How should it be instead? According to these prominent Church of God leaders:

> God's ministers received the everlasting gospel which they preach from the Lord. They receive it free. The anointing teaches them. They are "taught of God." . . . But all sects have their peculiar mark or doctrine with which they mark their subjects. They have erected preacher factories for the express purpose of marking their ministers with their particular mark.[3]

Being formally trained was announced as merely the process of a person being boxed in a human institution and tied by human thinking. It was understood to be a key element of the diseased backbone of the denominational system.

Probably it is most accurate to conclude that early pioneer leaders of the Church of God were not necessarily against education as such. But they certainly were against schools as they knew them. So much was this the case that the few leaders who had had the benefit of some formal education were known to hide the fact in order to retain status with the brethren. No wonder, then, that some Church of God preachers, once ordained to the ministry, actually burned all of their books (except the Bible) as a witness to their singular reliance upon God and his Word.

Such radical actions were a dramatic form of an earlier and related action of Warner. Sensing his call to the ministry and feeling that he must prepare to be a laborer in the Lord's harvest while it was yet day, he had cut short his studies at Oberlin College. He went home and for a season applied himself to prayer and Bible study, things he judged directly necessary to ministerial preparation.

It certainly was common for the pages of the *Gospel Trumpet* in those first decades after 1880 to carry very negative comments about education. Typically, however, the specific issue under attack was either substituting human learning for the grace of God, using schools for sectarian ends, or implying that the primary credential for effective Christian ministry could be issued by a school. Warner, for instance, argued that "as to men prescribing a course of study as a condition of preaching the Gospel, that is the vilest form of popery."[4] Seminaries were branded sectarian training grounds and hot beds of heresy. Colleges were seen as examples of human arrogance.

It can still be assumed, despite all such negative references, that education was seen as a potentially good and helpful thing. After all, persons like Warner and E. E. Byrum, while writing strong anti-educational articles, were at the same time building significant personal libraries and proving themselves diligent students of the Bible and related subjects. But there was little time to give attention to that potential. More important things were at hand. The gospel workers were hurrying around the country as a "flying ministry," rarely pausing long enough to establish congregations and certainly not stopping to build things as suspect as colleges.

In the early 1890s, however, at least a hint of changed attitude emerged. A home was organized in Grand Junction, Michigan, for the children of itinerant preachers. Regular classes in music, taught by A. L. Byers, and penmanship, taught by Jeremiah Cole, were conducted. But Warner envisioned something more, an "extensive educational project." Persons often had spoken and written to him about the possibility of a course in Bible study that would better equip them to labor in the Lord's vineyard. His heart had become stirred to make an effort in this direction. Even a simple curriculum was projected, with the possibility of three teachers. Suggested courses included Bible history and perhaps archaeology, the critical study of the New Testament, and lectures on prophecy, experimental and spiritual truth. Music and elocution would be added later.

Then came a major turning point for this idea and for the young movement itself. On the day of the first scheduled class in 1895 Warner fell ill. Within days he was dead. Soon Enoch E. Byrum became the new editor of the *Gospel Trumpet*, and he was quick to make clear his view and intent. He wrote:

> Some have asked if we have a theological school here. We answer, no. Neither do we expect to have. We have Bible readings and special faith meetings almost every evening which are wonderfully blessed of God by way of spiritual advancement and real soul food, and holiness is lifted up to the Bible standard.[5]

This hesitancy and almost defensiveness about the most modest of projected educational ventures reflected a widespread attitude in the young church movement. Lawrence Brooks, for instance, started his ministry in Arkansas in 1915. Soon he felt the need for some systematic preparation for his life's calling. The advice he got from older ministers was what he later recalled as the common attitude in those days: "Why fool around in school while souls are going to hell?" So it was in the early years.

This advice, however, came in the face of a growing discussion about the matter of the appropriateness of formal education for the work of Christian ministry, a discussion which, at least by 1912, included more than the status quo attitude of Byrum or the negative opinion received by Brother Brooks in Arkansas. While it is clear that the ranks of the young movement were filled with common folk with little or no school experience, it is also true that many of that first generation of leaders were educated persons by the standards of the time. On the one hand, both Warner and Byrum had attended college. According to the sociologist Dr. Val Clear, the first person representing the movement to preach in Anderson, Indiana, was a physician-turned-preacher and, at one time, forty-one of one hundred volunteer workers were school teachers.[6] Certainly the literary level of the early church publications suggests a highly literate leadership if not readership. On the other hand, most came from a rural background and had little inclination to use an educational approach to general church work. They often ranged from antagonism to apathy in their attitudes toward formal education. This situation made possible the development of a deep and difficult cleavage.

D. O. Teasley argued in the 1905 pages of the *Gospel Trumpet* that spirituality must be central and the apprentice method basic to the training of gospel workers. He wrote:

> Having recently seen some sad effects of human effort to train men and women for the ministry, I feel led to set forth the New Testament method of training those whom God has called to his work. . . . All theological institutes and missionary training schools are run too much on the theoretical plan, which is detrimental to spirituality and tends to fill the head and empty the heart. In ninety-nine cases out of a hundred a man goes into a missionary training school or theological institute a thousand times better fitted to win souls than he comes out. . . . It is the special duty of pastors to encourage, and care for, and instruct young workers. Good workers are the natural fruit of an able pastor and a spiritual church. . . . Workers are needed, but only those can be used who are able to convince the gainsayers, cast out devils, heal the sick, save souls, and perfect the saints."[7]

H. A. Brooks, in the 1912 pages of the same publication, developed a somewhat different thesis.

> To the ignorant and unlearned, the advantages of education are unknown. . . . Surely there is no evil in knowing how to do and say things well. Yet the unlearned maintain that it tends to pride and worldliness. This is not so; and indeed it is true that there are many more self-conceited people among the uneducated than there are among the learned. . . . There is talent in the church of God lying dormant in the hearts and minds of men and women, through lack of education. Education would give them tact and diligence to bring forth their talents to the rescue of the perishing world in good, plain, proper language in

the form of literature. . . . Men and women upon whom God lays his hand for the ministry in their youth must be public speakers, singers, readers, and writers all the days of their lives. . . . They should qualify themselves to meet ably every obligation and to fulfill properly each duty required of them in their calling."[8]

Such differing perspectives represented more than a temporary problem, something that would fade quickly once the Church of God movement got itself better established. T. Franklin Miller was the executive officer of the national Board of Christian Education for the period 1945-1966. He has reported that during those years there was still this same deep cleavage among ministers in the Church of God. Some leaders were committed to evangelism and some to education, with little appreciation shown for each other's views. Miller saw as a central feature of his own work in those years the attempt to bridge this gap. This gap, however, did not exist only in 1895 or 1915 or 1945-1966. Dr. Val Clear observed as recently as 1984:

> That discussion, that dichotomy, that choice never has been eliminated. It juxtaposes the movement between the false extremes of trusting God or trusting humankind, and much of Church of God institutional history and sociology consist of the ways in which we have dealt with that pseudo-issue.[9]

The Sunday School

With the Church of God having an essentially negative and yet increasingly mixed attitude toward formal education in those first decades following 1880, there also was a growing band of enthusiastic gospel workers who were anxious to be effective in their work. They did not see a systematic program of training as necessarily either a compromise with sectarianism or a flaunting of human pride in the face of God's grace and gifts for ministry. The need became more apparent and various kinds of educational experimentation emerged.

The Sunday school movement was very popular among United States churches during the early years of the Church of God movement. Being a highly structured, lay-oriented program often separated from the church bodies in whose buildings the classes met, Warner at first judged the Sunday school to be just another sectarian tool bringing more division to the body of Christ. Even so, he wrote in an 1885 editorial that "where there are a sufficient number of saints to hold a service especially for the instruction of the children and youths, there is no reason why such a service should not be held."

Classes of this kind became rather common and some evangelists experimented further by conducting children's meetings alongside their revivals. Special classes were held occasionally in the Gospel Trumpet Home. In fact, by 1892 there was a Sunday school in the Trumpet Home. The editorship of E. E. Byrum, while showing no enthusiasm for training schools, did support Sunday school work. By 1903 George L. Cole was writing a weekly column in the *Gospel Trumpet* entitled "The Sunday School Work." Given a concern about employing "Babylon's" literature and having judged the International Sunday School materials to have "such a taint of sectism and erroneous doctrinal views that it is not expedient to use them,"[10] by 1910 the Gospel Trumpet Company was publishing its own Sunday school quarterlies. The Sunday school avenue of education obviously had been accepted once it had been adapted to the concerns and perspectives of Church of God people.

The Missionary Homes

Also of increasing prominence during the early years of the Church of God movement was the growth and industrialization of cities. To these complex and problem-ridden settings came pioneer ministers of the Church of God who were burdened for the lost and the destitute. "Missionary homes" began to appear as teams of gospel workers conducted revival services, distributed literature, and helped the needy.

Probably the first such home was started in 1895 in Chicago by Gorham Tufts. It operated as a rescue mission, an evangelistic center, and later, under the leadership of E. A. Reardon, a place for a wide range of worship, service, and educational activities. Young people were attracted to this and similar urban homes. They had energy for service to others and they had needs of their own for growth and training.

In 1909, when F. W. Heinly was director of the missionary

home in New York City, he described the purposes of that and several other such homes:

> This home offers an excellent place for the training and instruction of young workers whom God has called. No prescribed course of lessons is given, but . . . a number of established ministers and workers are always here, ready to give the young worker the benefit of their varied experiences in gospel work, expound the Scriptures, and present the best methods for the study of the Bible, how to win souls and conduct meetings in the most effectual way.

Adam W. Miller, dean of Anderson School of Theology from 1953-1962, was once a participant in the "Study by Mail" program of the New York home. Albert F. Gray, later president of Warner Pacific College, helped with the beginning of the Missionary Home in Spokane, Washington, in 1904. Robert H. Reardon, president of Anderson College (University) from 1958-1983, was influenced deeply by life with his parents at the missionary home in Chicago.

By 1910 all of these missionary homes had begun to decline in strength and effectiveness. Some eventually were sold as apartment buildings while others became strong and permanent congregations. But whatever the end of each, all had performed in varying degrees a critical educational function. It was typical in these settings that informal counseling and study sessions became regular classes for enthusiastic young gospel workers. Several of the homes developed the name "Bible school" or "missionary training school," including the Kansas City Bible School and Spokane Bible School.

Some general softening of the harsh attitudes toward formal education had become evident. In a real sense the missionary homes were bridge institutions between what was slipping into the movement's past and what was about to come. They served for about a generation as the only existing "higher education system" of the Church of God.

It was becoming increasingly apparent that the "flying ministry" days were coming to an end. Now there was the need for establishing more settled congregations with traditional pastors. Converts needed stabilizing and nurturing. The deep bias against organization was lessening in the face of obvious need. The Trumpet Home and the publishing company itself had become formally organized, had finally settled permanently in Anderson, Indiana, in 1906 and was itself a significant if informal training base. Possibly (hopefully) all organization in the church's life was not sectarian after all! Slowly the door was opening both to the importance of education and even to the potential legitimacy of institutions of education being established to more systematically advance the work of the Lord.

A Crucial Year—1917

Between 1912 and 1917 a series of little booklets for ministers called *Our Ministerial Letter* appeared. Here was a communicating link among leaders in the church who needed more than the news and inspiration found in the *Gospel Trumpet*. They needed vigorous and substantive dialogue on topics central to their leadership responsibilities. They needed instruction.

The *Letter* included issues on "The Care of the Churches," "Financial Support of the Ministry," "Ministerial Relationships," and "Secrets of Success in Pastoral Work." Then came a sensitive, but vital concern. In the April 1917 issue of the *Letter* a foreword was written by J. W. Phelps. Very much as D. S. Warner had reported in 1895 when he was envisioning some systematic educational effort, Phelps reported:

> Young ministers and young men and women who are called to the ministry have been told again and again that they ought to prepare for their lifework. That the young people have realized the need of the best possible preparation is evidenced by the many earnest inquiries as to what they should study, what course of reading they should pursue. These questions are answered in this issue of *Our Ministerial Letter*.

Russell R. Byrum, then pastoring in Boston, authored the main entry in that issue, "The Preacher Among His Books."

Then in the August 1917 issue there appeared Byrum's "A Course of Study for Ministers." He wrote that "a minister who acts wisely may save an immortal soul for heaven, which is infinite gain; but by mistakes, neglect, or wrong-dealing with souls he may be responsible for their being lost in hell forever, and to miss heaven is an infinite loss." He went further by stating that there are two kinds of qualifications for this heavy responsibility of ministry. The *spiritual* comes first and is God-given. The *intellectual* comes also. It requires human effort and consists of knowledge relevant to ministry. This "information is obtained mostly from books." He concluded by observing that "we have no regular means of systematic training. It is not because we are opposed to preachers gaining knowledge, but the dangers and disadvantages that have sometimes attended training-schools have caused us to hesitate in adopting such means." Having laid the groundwork for justifying a course of study, he outlined a five-year reading plan with an annotated bibliography of suggested readings for each year.

That year was pivotal. In 1917 the General Ministerial Assembly of the Church of God organized formally in Anderson, Indiana. That same year, after about four decades of the movement's life, there finally was begun the first enduring institution of higher education in the Church of God. It would also be located in Anderson, Indiana, and R. R. Byrum would be a prominent figure in the early phase of its life. With all that had gone before, it should not be surprising that when the first school finally was launched, it would have to face periods of suspicion and strong opposition. Nonetheless, it was launched and it did survive as the first of several that would emerge later on.

Table 1 provides an overview of the founding of ten such institutions of higher education. The following chapters describe in brief the histories of these institutions.

Notes

[1] C.H. Forney, *History of the Churches of God* (Harrisburg, Pa.: Publishing House of the Churches of God, 1914), p. 566.

[2] *Gospel Trumpet,* Oct. 15, 1884, p. 2.

[3] Warner and Riggle, *The Cleansing of the Sanctuary,* Gospel Trumpet Company, 1903, pp. 379-380.

[4] *Gospel Trumpet,* Dec. 1, 1883.

[5] *Gospel Trumpet,* Dec. 26, 1895.

[6] Val Clear, *Where the Saints Have Trod,* (Chesterfield, Ind.: Midwest Publications, 1977), p. 20.

[7] D. O. Teasley, *Gospel Trumpet,* April 6, 1905, p. 1.

[8] H. A. Brooks, *Gospel Trumpet,* June 20, 1912, pp. 4-5.

[9] Val Clear, in *Educating for Service,* James Earl Massey, editor (Anderson, Ind.: Warner Press, 1984), p. 16.

[10] *Gospel Trumpet,* Jan. 1, 1903, p. 9.

Table 1
Overview of the Founding of Ten Institutions
Total Years of Service to the Church
As of 1988

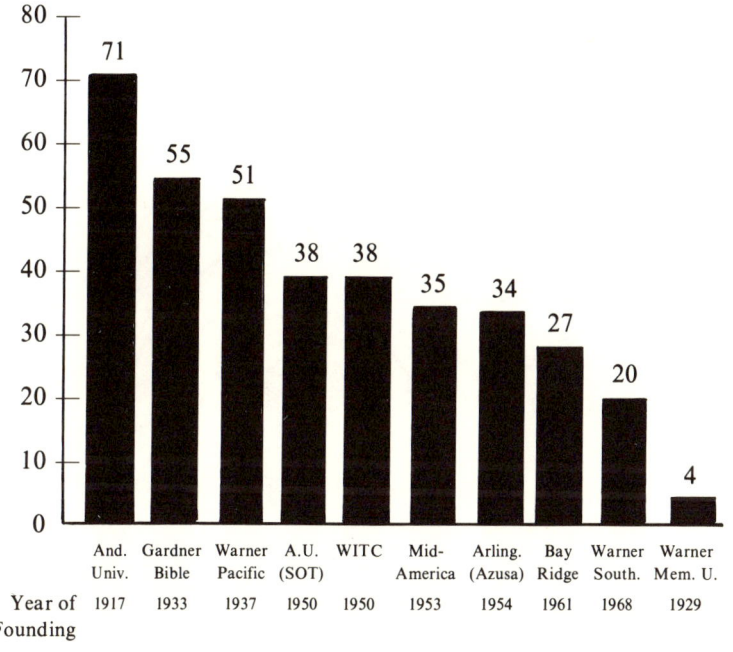

Chapter 3
The Story of Anderson University

In 1915 Adam W. Miller, a young convert from Baltimore, and several other aspiring ministers of the Church of God were attending a missionary convention at the Church of God Missionary Home in New York City. They confronted Joseph T. Wilson, general manager of the Gospel Trumpet Company in Anderson, Indiana, with a very important question: "When is someone going to provide young ministers with training for gospel work?" His answer brought them some hope. "The Gospel Trumpet Company is about to begin classes for workers and we would be glad to have you come to Anderson and join us." Such inquiries and the urging of Russell Byrum had convinced Wilson that he must act. And he was the kind of man who was willing to act in spite of the obstacles.

Those were difficult days financially for the Gospel Trumpet Company, and the general sentiment among Church of God people toward institutions of higher education, especially seminaries, was not very positive to say the least. But there had been signs of change in the attitudes of some, like the 1912 *Gospel Trumpet* article by H. A. Brooks titled "Advantages and Value of Education."[1] And the needs were so real that some persons were beginning to believe that there was a way despite the lack of financial resources.

An increasing number of competent leaders was needed. Evangelistic teams needed singers with trained voices. The company needed good writers, editors, and copy readers. There were young ministers like Adam Miller who wanted to learn about the Bible, the world, and their own ministerial calling, and there were persons writing to the *Gospel Trumpet* wanting to know if there were a Bible school where they could go to learn more about the message of the Church of God movement and how to preach and teach as ministers and gospel workers. It was time for something important to be born.

A Place to Begin

A reorganization of the Gospel Trumpet Company in June 1917 gave it the power to publish religious and moral literature, conduct homes for the aged, and maintain schools. It was time to act. Wilson, in a visionary act as general manager, prevailed on the members of the company to name a "managing committee" to begin an educational effort. Comprised of J. T. Wilson, H. A. Sherwood, J. E. Campbell, R. R. Byrum, and F. G. Smith, this committee of vigorous men went to work. They (primarily Byrum) arranged a course of study, selected textbooks, secured teachers, and advertised that a Bible training school was being opened in Anderson. It would operate as an educational department of the company with Wilson as principal.

The opening day for Anderson Bible Training School was October 2, 1917, in the Trumpet workers' home on East Fifth Street (to be the "Old Main" of the campus in later years). Space was available because the company had begun paying wages to workers and some families had moved to private quarters. There were five teachers: Russell R. and Bessie L. Byrum, H. C. Clausen, Mabel Helms, and H. A. Sherwood, with only Clausen and Helms full time.

The student body consisted of forty-nine persons who were workers at the company and students at night. Courses included Bible, music, English, homiletics, and public speaking. They were delivered as a series of lectures each Friday evening, October through May, with the overall two-year programs designed by Russell Byrum after he had studied the program of many schools.

As the catalog printed the following year clarified, "no attempt at mere intellectual development is intended." What was intended was the preparation of persons to fulfill their divine callings through the life of the church.

There was excitement, challenge, and caution being expressed in the school and across the church. Now there was a place to go! Classes were held in the Trumpet Home with dorm rooms on the floor above. Wilson continued to carry his regular responsibilities as general manager of the Gospel Trumpet Company. The school was modest, owned no property of its own, gave no formal recognition for work completed, and its faculty and students spent most of their time working at the Gospel Trumpet Company. But it was a definite and welcome beginning.

The first year of operation left some red ink on the books which some in the company thought could not be tolerated. War was raging in Europe and many of the young men left to take up arms. Some were not able to return as students for the school's second year and enrollment dropped. But there were those like Wilson and Russell Byrum who would not let it die. And since it continued to exist into the second year of the planned two-year curriculum, the 1918 General Ministerial Assembly decided to give it considerable attention. What the school might become if it did survive worried some of the ministers.

An increasing number of ministers had come to appreciate the need for such a training school. With only one or two exceptions there were no pastors in the Church of God who held college degrees, and there were many negative attitudes about "liberal" colleges and "sterile" seminaries. Naturally there was concern that the new school would introduce the standard titles and symbols of self-seeking and worldly sophistication and encourage reliance on credentials instead of the gifts of the Spirit. Some of the older pastors felt insecure with the prospect of a new generation of trained leaders. Many of the established leaders had more concerns than support for the whole educational project. So the GMA adopted the following in 1918 as appropriate guidelines for the future operation of Anderson Bible Training School:

1. We believe that such a school can be conducted to the glory of God and the welfare of the ministry and church if kept within certain bounds.
2. We believe that no effort should be made to create a sentiment to the effect that young ministers must attend this school in order to secure recognition.
3. It is our opinion that in many cases the education of ministers can best be obtained in those sections of the country where their ministerial work is to be done so that the practical can be more definitely combined with the theoretical. In other words, we do not believe that the Anderson Bible School should supercede or replace other training schools of the church.
4. Students should be left free to choose their own course of study from among such branches as the school provides.
5. No recommendation or diploma should be given any student. Satisfactory gradings in school constitutes no proof that an individual is called of God to preach the gospel. Hence every student must be left on his own responsibility so that he will not possess in this respect any authority proceeding from this school which will give him an advantage over those ministers who have not attended school. In the Church of God every minister must stand on his own merits and earn his place of responsibility whether educated or uneducated.
6. We believe that the training of ministers in this school should include more than their intellectual development along educational lines. The most prominent feature must be their personal development in spirituality, faith, and the gifts of the Spirit of God.

Already this young school had gained the attention of the Church of God at large, something to be typical of its coming relationship with the church. Among the first persons to complete its program in 1919, the first of many thousands to come, were such remarkable persons as: Anna Koglin, later to be a longterm teacher of German and Greek for the school; J. Frank Shaw, who gave his life as a missionary among the Indians of the American Northwest; and Louise Frederici, who became an assistant to the editor of the *Gospel Trumpet* in Germany.

Wilson had a tendency to begin more things than his management skills or the available resources could sustain. By 1923 he found himself forced out of the Gospel Trumpet Company and, heart broken, he chose to leave Anderson altogether. But he had made one move that would be crucial for the future stability of the young school. In February 1919 he wrote to John A. Morrison, a twenty-three-year-old pastor in Colorado, and encouraged him to consider teaching homiletics and helping with the administration of the school as assistant principal. Wilson had never met Morrison, but knew that he had some ministerial and teaching (public school) experience. Wilson was also encouraged by Russell Byrum, who had appreciated what Morrison had written for the *Gospel Trumpet*.

Morrison reflected years later on "the low estate of education in our movement" that "one such as I would be invited to have a place in the one and only educational institution operated by the church."[2] He had never been to high school, although he had attended normal school for several terms to prepare for teaching in Missouri. But he was given a place—and what a place it turned out to be! Linfield Myers, later to become a prominent business leader in Anderson and good friend of the school, said it was Morrison's "earthy quality, together with liberal helpings of his equally earthy humor, that helped him achieve greatness. . . ." He concluded, "If the leadership role of the new college had gone to someone of lesser human endowments back in 1919, this whole story might have been completely different."[3]

Soon church controversy was in the wind and the young school was in the middle of it. F. G. Smith, now editor of the *Gospel Trumpet* and author of very influential writings like the book *Revelation Explained,* was a powerful person in the Church of God. He had become to many persons the movement's spokesperson, its chief interpreter, the definer and protector of its treasures of truth. Nevertheless, some other persons wished for more democratic procedures in the church and even wanted to entertain points of view other than the so-called "standard" literature of the movement. Smith saw dangerous trends in these desires.

He was particularly disturbed by the fact that R. R. Byrum had begun using his Bible classes in the school as places to test various points of view, including alternatives to Smith's own interpretation of the New Testament Book of *Revelation*. The school was functioning as a stimulator of new ideas, sometimes even new ways of understanding the Church of God movement itself! In 1927 the popular Byrum left his editorial work at the company to cross the street and become full-time at the school where he was more appreciated and very much needed.

Byrum was needed because the curriculum had been extended and the school was growing. Despite the school's obvious limitations and the atmosphere of suspicion created by some, students generally were very enthusiastic and appreciative of their education. In 1924 Canadian graduate H. C. Gardner returned home burdened to begin a similar training effort (eventually Gardner Bible College). American graduate Nellie Olson returned as missionary to Jamaica to do the same (eventually Jamaica School of Theology).

In 1925 the Gospel Trumpet Company struck from its bylaws the portion providing the power to operate schools. The school sought a separate charter from the state of Indiana and the 1925 General Ministerial Assembly elected a fifteen-member board of trustees to govern a now independent institution. J. T. Wilson was named board chair. Morrison, who had become principal in 1923 when Wilson left, became the first president of the newly named Anderson Bible School and Seminary. The prohibition against granting degrees had been lifted in 1923 and made retroactive to the first graduates in 1919. Now, in addition to R. R. Byrum as vice-president and Oscar J. Flynt as treasurer, a major figure was to join President Morrison to complete the school's leadership team.

George Russell Olt, Church of God pastor-educator and dean of Wilmington College in Ohio, came in 1925 as faculty member and first dean. Though there were no dollar or prestige incentives that could be offered, Morrison convinced him that God had a big job to be done in Anderson and that he was the only person available to do it! It was Olt who would stand by Morrison's side for decades to come as an academic leader committed to excellence. "It was his dogged determination to bring strength and integrity to the educational program," recalled Robert H. Reardon, "that set the standard for a great deal of what has happened in higher education in the Church of God."⁴ With Morrison and Olt the school had a sterling pair of leaders with unusually complementary strengths. What was ahead would require all that they had.

Struggle for Survival, Identity, and Accreditation

Both the school and the church were now set to enter a period of severe trial. Each would face fundamental questions about its identity and mission and its proper relationship to the other. In addition, of course, the stock market crash of 1929 and all that followed in the nation kept mere survival a constant agenda item.

Dean Olt worked diligently to broaden the scope of the school's program by adding the liberal arts. This significant addition had the support of many of the school's graduates and prospective students who otherwise had to seek such "college" work in institutions not related to the church. To broaden the curriculum so, however, was quite an act of faith since the faculty had limited qualifications, there was no equipment for science courses, the total budget for 1926-27 was only $32,000, and student tuition was not even charged until 1925. But it was judged the right direction to go.

This addition of the liberal arts was authorized by the 1928 General Ministerial Assembly, but not without major opposition. What business, argued some, does the school have going beyond ministerial education? These critics argued further that the liberal arts would be an open door for worldliness. But the move was made and, accordingly, in 1929 the school's name was changed to Anderson College and Theological Seminary. A major statement of mission had been made by the school. Its legitimate arena of academic inquiry and professional preparation was potentially the whole spectrum of human knowledge and endeavor. The windows of learning were to be wide open. The college was going to be a "college" in the fullest sense of the word!

Back in 1919 F. G. Smith had published the book titled *The Last Reformation* which had emphasized that the Church of God movement was a fulfillment of biblical prophecy as understood by a particular interpretation of the Books of *Daniel* and *Revelation*. John Morrison and Russell Byrum disagreed and told Smith so.

Thus a basic question was posed openly: Did the movement's integrity rest in the fellowship of redeemed persons, or must there also be a common commitment to a particular understanding of biblical interpretation which understood the movement as prophetic fulfillment? Tension over this grew in the church. Byrum continued to explore various options in his classes. He raised questions about F. G. Smith's approach to interpreting prophetic literature and relied primarily on the Gospels and Epistles to lay a foundation for understanding Christian unity. Some showdown was coming and the school would be in the middle of it. It would be the clash between an educational institution prepared to test, learn, and grow and a sponsoring church which was questioning its willingness to be open and examine critically its own self-understanding. The crisis points were to come in the Anderson Camp Meetings of 1929 and 1934.

In 1929 there was a direct challenge to the orthodoxy of faculty member Russell Byrum on a range of issues. R. L. Berry, who had replaced Byrum as F. G. Smith's managing editor, brought the charges to the Board of Trustees of the school. A hearing, almost a heresy trial, was conducted over several days during the Anderson Camp Meeting. Although F. G. Smith was a chief witness against Byrum, Byrum's explanations and attitudes were generally acceptable to most. He was exonerated of "heresy," but caution was urged for his teaching. The trustees quickly drafted a statement of their belief, proposing that the faculty sign it as a way of avoiding any further and unwarranted accusations. Byrum saw this as unwise and himself now as a potential liability to the school. So he resigned to become a builder of homes in Anderson for the rest of his long life.

But the conflict was not over. Educational integrity had withstood a challenge, but the church had lost the skilled services of Byrum. Those sympathetic to Smith's views were frustrated and were to become more so the following year when the Publication Board refused to re-elect Smith to the editorship. That frustration would fester and soon be back for another confrontation.

It came in the 1934 Anderson Camp Meeting when President Morrison's ratification as college president was under consideration by the ministers. But between 1929 and 1934 opponents of both the idea of a church-sponsored liberal arts college and of reported "liberal" teachings at the college joined to attempt to force some changes. F. G. Smith, now pastoring in Akron, Ohio, and known to want control over the college within "last reformation" teachings and to mistrust John Morrison, used his major influence as a widely accepted spokesperson for the reformation movement.

Beginning with resolutions passed and circulated nationally by the Ohio Ministerial Assembly in 1933, a succession of resolutions were passed. They called for an end of the liberal arts college program and a return to a curriculum of "only such studies as are in keeping with a purely religious training school." Another influential Ohio pastor, C. E. Byers, wrote: "The College (liberal arts program) is not the work of the Church. Let the Church train and prepare her youth to preach the gospel. It is not the Church's business to run an institution to prepare folks to go out into the world in a business way."[5]

Secular truth, the concern of colleges, is always being debated and changing, so the college's critics argued vigorously. But true Bible unity, based on divinely revealed truth and taught in the movement's standard literature, is the only center to which all Christians can be brought. Secular "truths" and Bible truth, they concluded, should not mix in one institution expecting to be supported by the Church of God. Above all, this college in Anderson must not rule the pulpits; it is the pulpits of the church that must rule the college! There also were many charges of disloyalty to traditional teachings of the movement, with much of the focus on President Morrison whose term of office was coming up for reconsideration. Morrison and the liberal arts program were facing a major challenge.

The college responded with mailings, carefully worded responses to accusations in its *Broadcaster* publication, and personal appearances, explaining, defending, gently confronting. Morrison was sure of his ground and felt responsibility for thousands of the church's young people. Many letters of support flowed into Anderson.

When the showdown arrived in June 1934, the college trustees re-elected Morrison for another term as president despite the pressure to do otherwise. With a majority vote required for ratification in the General Ministerial Assembly, Morrison was subsequently ratified by a margin of only 243 to 231! A long meeting followed in an attempt to reconcile as many differences as possible for the sake of church unity. The movement had engaged in a major internal debate and would survive. So would John Morrison as president, Russell Olt as dean, and the liberal arts program to which both were committed. In later years Morrison and F. G. Smith were to be reconciled, finding joy together in their common commitment to Christ and his church whatever their differences in viewpoint on some things.

So a training school had begun, had matured into a small liberal arts college, had acquired strong executive and academic leadership, and had weathered major opposition from some very influential leaders within the church. Now the college had to find ways to build a future even while existing in the middle of a terrible economic depression. The first attempt at a major financial campaign had been launched by the college in 1929, but that turned out to be the year of the stock market crash. It was to be more than twenty years before the first new building could be erected.

The 1930s certainly were difficult years. An enrollment as low as ninety-one students was experienced in 1932-33. Faculty salaries were most inadequate and as the economy grew worse the faculty volunteered to have them lowered even more. Dollars and foodstuffs were collected for the students wherever they became available. An old college truck made trips to neighboring states to gather food from sympathetic farmers—once returning with five hundred quarts of sauerkraut from one church! The one large concrete block building, "Old Main," is all that there was. Dormitories, faculty apartments, classrooms, chapel, dining hall, carpenter shop, and laundry room were all housed under one roof. Dollars and students were scarce.

While on the road himself, President Morrison continued trying to convince doubting groups within the church of the wisdom of a church-related liberal arts college and of the urgent need to support the one in Anderson in very difficult times. He wrote in the *Gospel Trumpet:*

> Is anyone educated who has not been taught science,

music, history, literature, art, philosophy? Is anyone educated who has not been taught in religion? Can the state teach religion? Would we allow it? The fact is, brethren, if we hope to save our young people from shipwreck of faith during the process of their education we as a church must make it possible for them to receive that education amid Christian environments. . . . The State universities have so thoroughly secularized the educational process and divorced it from the religious program that unless the church colleges are enabled to carry on, leading religious thinkers are pretty well agreed that Christianity in America is doomed to be wiped out. . . . Anderson College and Theological Seminary . . . is having a terrific struggle to survive the present financial crisis. We must have help from those who believe in a spiritual program.[6]

In the middle of these difficulties there always were encouraging signs of success, growth, and hope. In 1930 alone significant persons like Carl Kardatzke, Amy Lopez, Earl Martin, D. S. Warner Monroe, and Esther Boyer Kirkpatrick Bauer were graduated. In 1932 the first liberal arts graduating class of twenty received Bachelor of Arts degrees. There was a director of intercollegiate athletics by 1934, with a team known as the "Tigers," a fitting symbol for a tenacious young college determined to prevail. And prevail it did. By 1937 enrollments were growing again and the Indiana Department of Education gave the college provisional accreditation for the education of public school teachers.

The year 1941, the College's twenty-fifth, was to be characterized by more than Jerry Hurst Reardon and Jack VanDyke being named best all-around woman and man on campus. President Morrison, despite his own struggle with the agonizing pain of arthritis, announced and worked toward four central and ambitious goals: Have five hundred students enrolled; remove the school's indebtedness; establish a loan fund for ministerial students; and achieve accreditation by the North Central Association.

In 1941-1942 the faculty consisted of twenty-one persons, fifteen of whom held at least a masters degree. It was the tragic year of Pearl Harbor and soon many of the male students began to leave school to join the war effort. The college was struggling to mature in a world in turmoil.

By 1946 many GI's were home from the war and coming to the college as nontraditional students. Student wives, small children, and temporary trailers became common around campus. With student enrollment growing and Jumpin' Johnny Wilson bringing national attention to the campus basketball team, the drive for full accreditation was on.

Morrison and Olt had worked systematically for several years to accomplish vital recognition by the academic world. They had given careful attention to improving business operations and the procedures related to student records. Faculty credentials and library holdings had been strengthened according to accreditation standards. Morrison insisted on a constructive wedding of education and religion. Olt was insistent on maintaining academic excellence. They were a great team.

Then, on March 27, 1946, in Chicago the North Central Association of Colleges and Schools voted to grant the accreditation, the first to any institution in the Church of God. It truly was a day of rejoicing!

An Anderson city newspaper the next day carried as a subtitle to its bold headline about the local college, "Institution takes place among academic leaders in country." It was a matter of community as well as campus pride. Generally the subtitle had meaning; practically, however, its realization was hindered by a genuine need for new campus facilities and instructional equipment. President Morrison announced the hope of building student dormitories, a library, a science building, a physical education plant, even launching a school of theology at the graduate level. This was more evidence of what the North Central examiners had said in their accreditation report: "The administration is forward looking."

Building on Strong Foundations

In the decade following accreditation there were many firsts for the college. There was the first football team, honorary societies, new building (student dorm Morrison Hall in 1950), and distinguished alumni awards, the first going to industrialist Vern Schield and missionary Daisy Maiden Boone. The faculty had grown by 1950-51 to forty-five full-time and eleven part-time persons and the student body was nearing one thousand. The curriculum had broadened to three degree programs at the undergraduate level (B.A., B.S., B.Th.) preparing persons for Christian ministry, music, teaching, and preprofessional training in a wide range of fields. It was a time of steady growth.

That growth included acts of conscience and courage. In the city of Anderson, for instance, the Chamber of Commerce became upset with Dean Olt and Dr. Candace Stone for their outspoken support of the labor, civil rights, and peace movements. But there were positive breakthroughs in community relations. With the help of Linfield Myers of Anderson Banking Company the successful financial campaign for the new campus library was made possible largely through the generosity and name of Charles E. Wilson, former Anderson industrial pioneer, president of General Motors and newly appointed Secretary of Defense in the cabinet of President Eisenhower. While relationships with the local business community had their awkward moments in the college's early decades, improvement had begun and would develop dramatically in the coming decades.

In the 1950s one could hardly have dreamed that the campus in the 1980s would have built Reardon Auditorium, cultural center of the area; have formed a partnership with Purdue University to serve specialized needs in the local labor force; be providing the two city hospitals with a large percentage of their trained nurses; have brought to town the annual summer training camp of a National Football League team. Slowly, from an isolated and even antagonistic relationship between the Church of God agencies in Anderson (including the college) and the city, change came. As the college developed and then demonstrated its sense of servant mission to the needs locally, the city and its people responded with increasing pride and support.

In the Church of God at large there was close relationship, constant interaction, and occasional tension with the college. The tension sometimes grew out of an anti-intellectualism in some quarters of the church, but more often from misinformation or from the suspicion and mistrust of "headquarters" and its bureaucracy, a critical tendency which has been part of the the history of the Church of God movement. Occasionally it came because the campus exercised leadership which was needed but not recognized or welcomed by all. An example in 1950 was the launching of the graduate School of Theology.

Although there never have been educational requirements for ministerial ordination in the Church of God movement, the years after World War II saw increasing numbers of young Church of God ministers seeking graduate degrees in seminaries like Oberlin Graduate School of Theology in Ohio (the same campus where D. S. Warner had studied briefly decades earlier). It became the strong conviction of leaders in Anderson like Harold Phillips, Gene Newberry, Adam Miller, Earl Martin, Franklin Miller, Robert Reardon, John Morrison, and Russell Olt that the Church of God should provide such graduate education on the Anderson campus. Morrison, having himself spent time in 1942 at Oberlin as guest of seminarian Robert H. Reardon, recommended the idea to the college Board of Trustees in 1946. Its desired nature and likely cost were explored and tested by a Board committee for two years. When the questions were all addressed and the final decision made, plans were developed to actually launch the new school in October 1950 as a graduate division of the institution.

Dr. Earl Martin was the first dean. As that first term began there were thirty-five students and one full-time faculty member, Dr. Gene Newberry. The three-year Bachelor of Divinity degree was to be offered and all standards and structures being put in place had in view eventual accreditation by the Association of Theological Schools. There was no additional funding from the church for this new venture, so the college underwrote all costs and housed the operation, including the beginnings of a new and separate library, on an upper floor of Old Main. Invaluable assistance came from the Indianapolis-based Lilly Endowment to enable the adding of a new faculty position each year until a full teaching staff eventually was in place.

Soon Dr. John W. V. Smith and Miss Delena Goodman were on the graduate faculty. Dr. Adam Miller became dean in 1953. By 1955 there were approximately seventy-five graduate students, twenty-one graduate degrees already granted and election to the status of Associate Member of the Association of Theological Schools. It was an excellent beginning!

The end of the 1950s was a time of major transition for the institution. The several new buildings, including a library (1957), women's residence hall (1958), the School of Theology building (1961), and gymnasium (1962), gave a very different appearance to the campus as Russia's launching of Sputnik opened the era of space and gave a different appearance to the world. Death claimed leading campus figures like Dean Olt (1958), Carl Kardatzke (1959), John Kane (1960), and others. There were financial problems and significant opportunities. President Morrison retired in 1958 after thirty-five years as chief executive officer and, with Dean Olt's death that same year, a new executive team was needed to carry on the long tradition of forward looking and faithful leadership.

The heavy mantle fell on Robert H. Reardon as president and Robert A. Nicholson as dean in 1958. It was the beginning of a new and effective partnership that would last for one-quarter of a century. But it was a beginning marked by a rich continuity with the past. Reardon, who had grown up around the campus almost from the school's opening year and who had returned to the campus in 1947 to be the president's assistant, later reflected: "It has been helpful to have known the college in its infant days of struggle and to have caught during my high school years the dream of its future shared by Dr. Morrison and Dean Olt."[7] Nicholson, who first came from Minnesota as a student in 1940 and then had become a faculty member and chair of the music department, was to have a very long and distinguished tenure with the institution, serving as dean of the college for twenty-five years and then as president beginning in 1983.

Six major institutional objectives had emerged from the work of the President's Study and Planning Commission which Morrison had established and Reardon had chaired. These objectives, significant directional priorities for the new administration in 1958, were basic concerns: exhalt the spiritual and train for responsible Christian citizenship; improve instruction; attract qualified students; raise faculty salaries; build and conserve the physical plant; and broaden the base of financial support for the institution. It was a big challenge indeed, but there were good foundations on which to build and the builders were skilled, experienced, and dedicated.

The eventful years 1958-1983 saw the Reardon-Nicholson administrative team lead, build, conserve and bring increasing maturity to every aspect of campus life. Institutional student enrollment approached the two thousand mark in 1971-72 and was to remain quite stable despite the volatile forces affecting the world of American higher education. New campus facilities were provided to accommodate the growth in student population and the increasing range of academic and support programs. A men's residence hall and a science building were completed in 1964. In 1967 a dormitory, apartments for married students, and additional athletic facilities were completed. The next year the historic and beloved "Old Main" was demolished so that Decker Hall, a major administrative-academic complex, could be built on the site in 1968-1970. Then Olt Student Center was doubled in size and a natatorium was erected. A beautiful, modern campus was becoming a reality.

The Vietnam war years brought turmoil to the nation and some related tension to the campus. President Reardon, a strong leader determined to retain the distinctiveness and integrity of the campus, both applauded the sensitive consciences of students—he always loved students and was loved by them—and held the line when they wanted to go too far (like wanting to abolish mandatory chapel/convocation attendance). He said in 1972 that he hoped "the turbulent 1960s with their rebellious, impatient, tuned-in, turned-on, tell-it-like-it-is, revolutionary approach to the world" were over and that the college would "recover something of the quiet thoughtfulness and balanced judgment which are marks of civil and refined people."[8] The campus had not burned as many had, but it had not escaped the strain of those difficult years for the nation.

One of the significant and creative programmatic developments during those volatile years was the beginning of the TRI-S (Student Summer Service) program in 1964. With Norman Beard, then Dean of Students, as its skilled administrator this program began exporting student labor and love all over the world in international learning and service experiences. Another significant development came in 1972 when the Center for Pastoral Studies began under the leadership of Dr. Barry Callen. It was the special unit of the School of Theology to coordinate the professional development of ministerial students on campus and to be the agency for accrediting, recording, and sometimes sponsoring programs of continuing education for active ministers (more than one thousand ministers soon became involved nationwide). A third such development was the creation in 1973 of the Center for Public Service under the leadership of Dr. Larry Osnes. It supported selected students from many major fields of study who desired assistance in preparing to serve the public effectively through utilizing their own careers as service opportunities.

Major academic programs on campus continued to expand and gain national recognition. New accreditations were granted by the National Council for the Accreditation of Teacher Education in 1963, the Association of Theological Schools in 1965 (related to the School of Theology), the National League of Nursing, the National Association of Schools of Music in 1974, and the Council on Social Work Accreditation in 1979. The Master of Religious Education degree was added in the School of Theology in 1967 and other specialized masters programs began there in 1973.

The campus administration was active and innovative throughout these years. Many highly gifted and credentialed persons were brought into the life of the institution and given the encouragement to grow and be creative. President Reardon identified a central reason for this growth: "Young Christians and their parents want a school that has standards of behavior, that has a framework of faith, a religious root system, but where there is a strong academic program, a strong sense of freedom to think, to explore within a sense of community where people come to know one another and participate in one another's lives." [9]

Relationships between the campus and the Church of God remained vital. Thousands of young persons had come to the campus from local congregations and then had taken their places of leadership and service across the nation and the world. Significant financial support came to the campus annually from the church's World Service budget. Many students who had gone abroad first on a TRI-S project began moving into the ranks of the full-time missionaries sent by the church. Graduates of the School of Theology were filling more and more church leadership positions.

By 1971, however, some issues in the School of Theology had to be faced. The enrollment was low, the faculty aging and the church, maintaining no educational requirements for ordination, apparently was satisfied to allow the campus to carry the full financial responsibility of this, the one seminary of the church. It was time to explore program and even affiliation options.

The Board of Trustees authorized: (1) new degree programs (Master of Ministry and Master of Arts in Religion) which required less completion time and gave more specialization potential than the standard Master of Divinity degree; (2) the beginning of the Center for Pastoral Studies which would allow new stress on the internship and continuing education aspects of ministerial education; and (3) affiliation with the evolving Foundation for Religious Studies in nearby Indianapolis which would enable student program enrichment opportunities in the seminaries involved.

The church's 1972 General Assembly, pleased with some of these developments, nonetheless had some objections, particularly to the affiliation arrangement which was seen by many ministers as an inappropriate way to educate future Church of God ministers. When the debate had subsided, resolutions passed by majority vote called for: (1) an end to this affiliation which seemed a contradiction of the Movement's heritage; (2) the naming of a special study on a plan for continuation of a Church of God seminary responsible more directly to the General Assembly; and (3) the launching of a multi-year study by the Commission on Christian Higher Education on theological and ministerial education in the Church of God. For the first time the School of Theology, born and reared by the Anderson campus, was being examined closely, disciplined, and even adopted by the church at large. This process had its pain, pitfalls, and real potential.

The 1973 General Assembly heard its study committee report that a free-standing seminary separated from Anderson University, a model advocated by some, was not desirable functionally or feasible economically. Instead, the committee recommended and the Assembly agreed that the School of Theology should receive separate and increased World Service support, its Church of God students should receive new scholarship funding from the church, and its dean, still to be elected by the campus Board, should be ratified by the Assembly as was the campus president. Dr. Barry Callen was so ratified as the seminary's new dean in 1974, succeeding the retiring Dr. Gene Newberry, and student enrollment grew dramatically from 68 in 1974 to 188 by 1977. In 1975 the Adam W. Miller Chapel and library addition were added to the School of Theology building. Exciting days had arrived!

Another tension-filled but eventually constructive period for the campus was 1980-81 when an "open letter" sent to ministers by a pastor charged the college with yielding to liberalism and humanism in certain of its teachings and practices. The 1981 General Assembly received a major report from the campus Board of Trustees in which charges were addressed and stances taken. This well-prepared report cleared the air and left no doubt that the college was committed both to the church and to the integrity of an open educational process. Obviously the Board, as it had been elected to do by the Assembly, was now knowledgable and intending to govern the college's affairs effectively.

It is important to realize that the times of tension between church and campus often were reflections of struggles within the larger Christian church and certainly between differing groups within the Church of God. Such struggles easily focused on the Anderson campus because of its visibility, central geographic location, strategic influence, and many contact points with the life of the church. The college has played a pivotal role in the general development of the Church of God movement and even of several of the church's other institutions of higher education. In 1981, for instance, the college granted honorary doctoral degrees to four of its own graduates of earlier years, persons who had gone on to make major leadership contributions to sister Church of God colleges. They were: Milo Chapman (B.Th., 1939) from Warner Pacific College; Walter Doty (B.A., 1939) from Mid-America Bible College; Leslie Ratzlaff (B.A., 1940, B.Th., 1941) from Warner Southern College; and Horace Germany (B.Th., 1944) from Bay Ridge Christian College.

Organizing for the Future

The year 1983 would mark another new beginning. Robert Reardon retired from the presidency after twenty-five years and his dean of all those years, Robert Nicholson, was elected by the

Board to become the third president of the institution. Nicholson had deep roots in higher education, the Church of God, and the history of the college. In his inaugural address of October 1983 he expressed his profound debt for leaders of the past and his intent not necessarily always "to stand where they stood" but rather "to stand on their shoulders, to seize the strength of their steadfastness, to peer further out into the unknown. . . ."

Excellent foundations had been laid; now it was time to organize for the demanding times that lay ahead. It would not be easy in the face of declining numbers of eighteen-years-olds in the country, reductions of student financial aid from the government, and aggressive recruitment by public institutions of higher education with low tuition charges. It would take new efforts and new resources to retain the distinctiveness of the institution, face sharply rising costs, yet remain affordable for those students, particularly from the Church of God, who would want this special alternative in higher education. In 1946 a local Anderson newspaper may have been premature in announcing at the time of initial accreditation that the "institution takes place among academic leaders in country." The 1990s, however, could bring substance to such a bold assertion if the campus could find ways to meet these challenges.

Nicholson made good use of his year as president-elect. When he assumed the presidency in the summer of 1983 he had put in place a formal mission statement accompanied by eight institutional goals for the years 1983-1987. The goals addressed campus distinctives, student enrollment aspirations, personnel development needs, a major growth goal for the endowment of the institution, and so on. It was time for purposeful and disciplined action.

The president reorganized the administration and, with the help of Dr. Barry Callen, who moved from the deanship of the School of Theology to that of the college, he reorganized the college into three schools to accomplish a level of academic and personnel administration better suited to the future. New commitment was made to the cruciality of the liberal arts program after the completion of an intense review of its philosophy and curricular structure.

Working closely with Board chair Ronald Fowler, the president proposed a reorganization of the manner in which the Board did much of its work. The Board adopted the new plan in the belief that it would increase its direct involvement in informed campus governance. The institution joined the Christian College Coalition and soon was recognized as one of its more prominent members nationally. Attempts were made to devise an effective campus planning process. A systematic and efficient way of setting annual priorities was sought for in an increasingly complex institution, using the best wisdom and the wisest allocation of available resources. After some frustration and excellent consultant assistance, a strategic planning process finally was put in place in 1987.

In 1985 President Nicholson launched a five-year "Campaign for Anderson College" which sought $25 million for the heart of the institution, primarily its students, faculty, and academic programs. With chief financial and development officer Ronald Moore assuming leadership and Bill and Gloria Gaither co-chairing a national campaign cabinet, significant funding was sought for endowment of student financial aid, faculty development, key academic programs, and a major expansion of library space, including computer automated modernization of its services. The stress on endowment was seen as essential if the future was to be marked by stability and excellence. By the end of 1987, with two of the five years completed, approximately $12 million already had been committed, with groundbreaking for the library project anticipated in the summer of 1988.

The campus continued its tradition of innovation as it sought to fulfill its stated mission of being "an institution of Christian higher education at its best." The Krannert Fine Arts Center had been erected in 1979 to house the music and art programs and provide general classroom space. In 1984 Reardon Auditorium was opened as a worship, cultural, and entertainment center for the campus and the city (local citizens and businesses shared in the cost by providing 1.7 of the 5.5 million dollars in a time of high local unemployment!). The campus and its fine facilities had become host to activities as diverse as a symphony orchestra, special olympics, and the training camp of a National Football League team (Indianapolis Colts). The undergraduate college was increasing in its attractiveness to young persons with church backgrounds other than the Church of God. The graduate School of Theology continued to serve graduates from all colleges related to the Church of God and from many others as well (see table at the end of this chapter).

The School of Theology, under the leadership of Dean Jerry Grubbs, developed its Florida extension program on the Warner Southern College campus while the Center for Pastoral Studies, directed by Dr. James Bradley, continued to broaden its services to ministers nationwide. After several years of offering the Associate degree in Nursing, the first Bachelor of Science in Nursing degrees were granted. The campus entered a unique and widely heralded relationship with Purdue University, enabling Purdue to offer Associate degrees in technical fields to nontraditional students in the Anderson area. The first of these Purdue degrees were granted in 1987 as part of Anderson's commencement ceremony, a signal event in a partnership of public and private institutions formed to serve most efficiently a real public need. Also in 1987 Anderson initiated its own adult education program for a range of local persons not served by Purdue's technology-oriented programs.

Even though the 1980s were difficult years in higher education, including significant problems experienced by all of the other Church of God colleges, Anderson remained relatively stable in enrollment, innovative in programming, and well managed financially. It began to serve some new constituencies without violating its distinctive mission. It sought to strengthen faculty salaries and obtain expensive instructional equipment without raising student costs beyond affordability. It was seeking to retain that precious quality of community, that atmosphere of personal caring, sharing, and learning together in the midst of both the diversity of ideas and vocational goals and the unifying factor of Christian faith.

Then in May 1987 the Board of Trustees determined that it was appropriate and timely to change the institutional name to Anderson University. This would reflect more accurately an institution that had come to comprise a strong liberal arts college with some sixty majors, a graduate School of Theology with a range of masters degree programs, a new division of adult continuing education, and the possibility of new masters programs not related to ministerial training. In President Nicholson's recommendation to the Board on behalf of this change he stressed that, "acknowledging God as the source of truth and wisdom, we seek unification in a Christian faith perspective . . . *uni*versity, unity in the midst of diversity, and not 'multiversity' as is often seen today in higher education."[10] This name change, effective September 1987, was a result of an institutional maturing with deep roots in its own history and longstanding commitments; it also was an act of openness to the widening doors of the future and a sign of resolve that those doors would be entered with creativity and courage.

Notes

[1] *Gospel Trumpet,* June 20, 1912, pp. 4-5.

[2] John A. Morrison, *As the River Flows* (Anderson College Press, 1962), p. 126.

[3] Linfield Myers, *As I Recall: The Wilson—Morrison Years,* (Anderson College Press, 1973), p. 78.

[4] Robert H. Reardon, *The Early Morning Light* (Anderson, Indiana: Warner Press, 1979), p. 54.

[5] Letter to A. T. Rowe of the Gospel Trumpet Company, quoted by Norman Beard, "Anderson College: Its Contribution to the Training of the Ministry of the Church of God" (Anderson School of Theology Masters Thesis, 1958), pp. 30-31.

[6] Issue of February 12, 1931, p. 19.

[7] From published reflections made by President Reardon to the Board of Trustees on the occasion of his retirement, April 1983.

[8] As quoted by John W. V. Smith, *The Quest for Holiness and Unity* (Anderson, Indiana: Warner Press, 1980), p. 389.

[9] As quoted in *Vital Christianity,* September 11, 1983, p. 11.

[10] "A Perspective and Recommendation to the Anderson College Board of Trustees from Robert A. Nicholson, President," May 15, 1987, p. 3.

Table 2

Anderson University (Anderson, Indiana)

Institutional Names:
- 1917-1925 Anderson Bible Training School*
- 1925-1929 Anderson Bible School and Seminary
- 1929-1964 Anderson College and Theological Seminary
- 1964-1987 Anderson College
- 1987-   Anderson University

*Prior to 1925, the school operated as a department of the Gospel Trumpet Company.

Accreditations:
  1946—North Central Association of Colleges and Schools
  1963—National Council for the Accreditation of Teacher Education
  1965—Association of Theological Schools
  1974—National League of Nursing
  1974—National Association of the Schools of Music
  1979—Council on Social Education

Chief Executive Officers:
  1917-1923 Joseph T. Wilson
  1923-1925 John A. Morrison (principal)
  1925-1958 John A. Morrison (president)
  1958-1983 Robert H. Reardon
  1983-   Robert A. Nicholson

Chief Academic Officers (College):
  1917-1925 (Chief Executive Officers)
  1925-1958 George Russell Olt
  1958-1983 Robert A. Nicholson
  1983-1988 Barry L. Callen
  1988-   A. Patrick Allen

Chief Academic Officers (School of Theology):
  1950-1953 Earl L. Martin
  1953-1962 Adam W. Miller
  1962-1974 Gene W. Newberry
  1974-1983 Barry L. Callen
  1983-1988 Jerry C. Grubbs
  1988-   Barry L. Callen (acting)

Current Chair of Governing Board:
  1981-   Ronald J. Fowler

Table 3

Sources of New Seminarians

The School of Theology of Anderson University is the only seminary sponsored by the Church of God. Its students are graduates of many institutions, including those related to the Church of God. The following lists the number of first-time seminarians who came each year to the School of Theology as graduates from an institution associated with the Church of God.

Year:	1981	82	83	84	85	86	87
Undergraduate Institution:							
Anderson University	21	19	25	23	25	25	16
Azusa Pacific University	0	1	1	0	1	0	1
Bay Ridge Christian College	0	0	1	0	0	0	0
Gardner Bible College	1	2	3	3	0	1	0
Mid-America Bible College	3	6	5	5	3	13	1
Warner Pacific College	2	2	3	5	6	2	3
Warner Southern College	10	6	6	7	3	3	1
Totals:	37	36	44	43	38	44	22

Of all new seminary students, the *percent* who had graduated from one of the institutions associated with the Church of God	63	59	72	55	58	56	52

UNDER GOD
IN QUEST FOR TRUTH

Chapter 4
The Story of Arlington College

The early 1950s in the Church of God in Southern California were years marked by an evangelistic zeal and a missionary spirit. The church was alive. It was a time of learning, growing, and serving. Realizing that training was needed to maximize the service gifts given by God, soon a lay academy was organized. In the Whittier church, with area pastors Rev. Carl Swart as dean and Rev. Clifford Tierney as registrar, the Southern California School of the Bible began operating on thirteen successive Tuesday evenings between February and May 1953. Every church school teacher in the congregations of the Los Angeles area was urged to attend with the promise that the school would "strive for academic proficiency, but the spiritual emphasis and personal evangelism will remain pre-eminent.... At no time will the academic life supercede the spiritual life of the student." About two hundred persons participated enthusiastically.

Between September and December of 1953 another such educational effort operated on thirteen successive Monday and Tuesday evenings in the East Los Angeles Church. This time it was called California Christian College with David Martin, layman in the Pomona church, acting as president and C. Herbert Joiner, Jr., pastor of the Whittier church, acting as dean. This "college" program continued the previous lay-leadership training, but it operated on two levels by adding some actual college-level education.

The result of such training efforts was enough excitement and momentum that the young evangelist, Rev. Maurice Berquist, was called from his seminary training in Louisville, Kentucky, to become the executive secretary of the Association of the Church of God of Southern California. He arrived in 1954, bringing his new bride and much youthful enthusiasm of his own. He has called what he found a "fantastic program" involving nearly three hundred committed Christians seeking to grow through these educational efforts. Soon he was pastoring the Arlington church, broadcasting on the radio in Los Angeles, and stimulating missionary interest in every way possible.

In the spring of 1954 the educational program began another term, this time maturing into a daytime program in more of a campus setting. Camp Anza, an old Army camp near Riverside, had been purchased by the area churches and turned into a campground. It now became the site of classes which still stressed evangelism and missionary preparation. Several students came from across the United States and Canada to be part of what now was being called World Evangelism Institute. Martin and Joiner continued as president and dean.

The first issue of the little publication *World Evangelist* sought to spread across the continent the news of this most recent development. Letters praising the intent and early success of this enhanced program came back quickly. In the publication's second issue a few of these letters were reproduced, including those from ministers O. L. Johnson in Warsaw, Indiana; Kenneth Prunty in Smith Center, Kansas; and Gordon Schieck in Camrose, Alberta, Canada.

Missionary zeal was very much alive in Southern California. An educational program had begun as a way to bring substance to that zeal and the word was getting out by the summer of 1954. The ministers of the Association of the Church of God of Southern California met in the Whittier church and voted overwhelmingly to expand the training program into a full-time college. Enthusiasm ran high even though finances were limited and few of the pastors were experienced in operating a college.

When the Study Commission on Christian Higher Education of the Church of God met in Anderson, Indiana, in June 1954, the Association of the Church of God of Southern California was represented by C. Herbert Joiner, Jr., Maurice Berquist, Herschell Rice, Albert Kempin, Mark Denton, and John Neal. The proposed new college in California was discussed at length. Questions were raised by representatives of existing colleges about whether the Church of God had the strength to support another college. There was some stress on the difficulties inherent in such a proposed venture. Finally, given the commission's proposed criteria for starting a new college in the church and its assumption that these criteria could not be met in time to launch a new college by the fall of 1954, the commission recommended delay, further study, and another report of findings to the commission.

Historian John W. V. Smith in *The Quest for Holiness and Unity* (p. 340) recalled that in the 1940s and 1950s there were several "regional enthusiasms" calling for new colleges. The national Commission on Christian Higher Education of the Church of God, formed in part to help control the development of excessive competition with established schools, related to circumstances such as the possible emergence of Arlington College. "With little assistance and considerable discouragement from the powerless commission," wrote Smith, "this school began nevertheless."

Arlington College, choosing not to delay, opened its doors in the fall of 1954 with about fifteen students, including the young Gerald Marvel from Oklahoma who had been encouraged to come by Rev. Berquist. A central aim was "the inculcation of vital missionary vision and passion for worldwide service." Standard Bible courses were offered and it was suggested that students could supplement their work with liberal arts courses through the nearby University of California at Riverside or Riverside College.

Why had this educational effort emerged? Partly it was because of the encouraging local and even nationwide response to the World Evangelism Institute. But it no doubt was helped by the growing influx of people into the Southern California area and by a regional concern. It was a long way to Portland, Oregon, or Anderson, Indiana, where the established colleges of the church were located and air travel was not yet common. The established colleges had not developed regional outposts to serve regional needs. It was judged that in this case area needs justified an area response. Further, California had an extensive and, for students, very inexpensive network of institutions of higher education that could supplement what seemed beyond Arlington's own resources. So Arlington had begun.

The new college was near industry, which brought hope for student employment, and new housing developments where the practical opportunities for meeting spiritual need were many. Gerald Marvel recalled that the college really began as a child, cared for tenderly by local Church of God congregations. Meals and bedding were brought in for students. The campus, operating on the Arlington campground property, provided the atmosphere of a small, close family pioneering for God.

In those first years faculty and students felt a sense of urgency and were dedicated to a compelling mission. President Joiner provided the heart of the venture. He modeled a rich blend of evangelistic fervor and scholarly integrity. And with him was Dean Fred Shackleton who had come from Pacific Bible College to Arlington in its first year of existence. He believed deeply in the mission of the new college and gave freely of himself. By 1958 there were fifty-seven students (twenty-one from California, nine from Ohio, five each from Kansas and Oklahoma, two each from Colorado, Indiana, Michigan and New York, one each from six other states and three from outside the United States). This information is from the *Aletheia,* the college's yearbook publication. The total annual enrollment, including all part-time students, was somewhat higher.

The story of how the nine students migrated all the way from Ohio was probably typical. This group came from the Newton Falls congregation. It began when young Jack Winland wanted to go into the ministry, didn't have his high school diploma, and heard about Arlington College through the ministry of Maurice Berquist. Although most of its students held high school diplomas, Arlington accepted Winland despite his educational deficiency. Winland's experience at Arlington was good and in the summer of 1958 he and the gospel team of John Adams and Doug King visited the Newton Falls youth group. By August several other young people were on their way to California, including Norm and Marge Patton who had just been married and drove across the country even though Norm was only seventeen years old! In another year still others followed from Newton Falls.

These years were characterized by explorations designed to find a permanent location and a respectable accreditation status for the college. During 1954 Arlington attempted a bold step forward by laying plans for buying a new site in Riverside that might even have included some merger possibility with Pacific Bible College. But neither ever materialized. PBC decided not to proceed and Arlington was not able on its own to capitalize on the opportunity.

In 1956 Berquist left the area for a pastorate in Florida. He later recalled that after the collapse of the merger talks with PBC, circumstances pressed Arlington not to attempt building a four-year college and shouldering alone all the accreditation requirements. Dewayne Bell recalled that by 1958 the regional accrediting association had led Arlington to believe that its best hope was in an affiliation with an accredited institution. At the same time some questions were being raised within certain quarters of the Church of God about the need and viability of another college. So the future seemed clear. Arlington would need to seek some cooperative arrangement in the Los Angeles area. Meanwhile, it also decided to seek recognition and support as a national agency of the Church of God.

On December 6, 1957, President Joiner officially informed the Executive Council of the Church of God that, by direction of the Arlington College Board of Trustees and with the support of the Association of the Church of God of Southern California, "Arlington College hereby requests . . . admission into the family of agencies which receive regular support through World Service funds." Joiner stated that since its inception in 1954 the college had done "everything possible to achieve and maintain harmony and unity with all the Church's general agencies." He reported that in that space of time the churches of Southern California had both carried the financial load imposed by Arlington's educational program and maintained their previous level of World Service support. On February 19, 1958, the Executive Council reviewed this request, assured Arlington College of its interest and concern and forwarded the matter to the Study Commission on Higher Education. In the commission meeting of February 21, 1958, the matter was addressed for information and clarification. No action was taken.

After years of temporary status the June 19, 1958, meeting of the Commission on Christian Higher Education was its first as a permanent body of the General Ministerial Assembly. In accord with its new bylaws it was determined that Arlington College (along with Alberta Bible Institute in Canada and Gulf Coast Bible College in Texas) be invited to participate as an "associate" member. At the April 10, 1959, commission meeting convened at Pacific Bible College in Portland, President Joiner was officially seated as Arlington's delegate.

There was considerable discussion in that meeting about Arlington's proposed move to Long Beach. Then came the time for considering Arlington's request for membership in the Executive Council and the Division of World Service. The final motion adopted was a judgment to be conveyed to the Executive Council. It included appreciation for the cooperative attitude of Arlington, a recounting of the requirements for Executive Council membership by any agency, and a reminder that "any institution should be expected to demonstrate wide acceptance and approval by the church and some history of success in achieving stability and purposes consonant with the policies and program of the other general agencies of the Church of God before being invited to participate in the distribution of World Service funds." Making the assumption that Arlington had not yet qualified for such participation, it promised to keep the Executive Council informed of Arlington's future progress.

That progress was being sought through an informal cooperative arrangement with a state institution in Southern California. Joiner explained the plan to the commission in its January 1960 meeting. Long Beach State College had a dean with Church of God background who promised cooperation and Rev. Wilford Denton pastored the College Park Church of God congregation located just blocks away from that state campus. Arlington College decided to buy five acres of prime property, part of an old ranch on the hill just behind the state campus. In the summer of

1960 Rev. Denton opened his church for college use while a new building was constructed (mostly with donated labor).

Moving the campus brought its difficulties. Gerald Marvel, who graduated in 1960, did not feel good about abandoning "our family" out in Arlington for this very different setting. President Joiner, now seriously ill, initially supported the move, but near its time he had difficulty handling a decision of this magnitude, became fearful, and withdrew his support. The executive committee of the college's board tried to reverse the board's decision to move. When this attempt failed, the executive committee resigned and a leave of absence was granted to the president. The college did move, but, according to Everett Richey, "the community of spirit that had founded the college was now fractured. It was never restored."

The illness, absence, and later death of Joiner was a great loss to the college. He had been a man of vision who was an effective scholar, fund-raiser, and encourager of students. His departure created a leadership vacuum at a critical time. The beloved Earl Martin brought temporary leadership during 1960-61. Rev. George Ramsey assumed the presidency in 1961, but in 1963 he left for a faculty position at Anderson College.

The basic Long Beach plan was that an Arlington student would take a program of liberal arts courses at the state school and a program of religious studies at Arlington, often simultaneously. It was thought to be an academically strong plan and a good stewardship of resources. After one year of residence in California a student qualified for very low resident tuition rates at the state college. So it was hoped that students would come from across the country. The liberal arts program was strong and, according to Ramsey, the secular dangers were recognized, but it was thought that any negative influences could be counteracted by the Arlington faculty. It was made clear that "the college will continue to operate absolutely as a Church of God institution." It was announced that "Arlington College can successfully fulfill the purposes and aims of a Christian liberal arts college, but will be spared the prohibitive cost of actually executing a liberal arts program on its own campus."

Arlington's relationship with Long Beach State College was very informal. Arlington students took accredited liberal arts courses at the state college and had their records transferred to Arlington to supplement the religious studies, thus comprising the four-year Arlington program. It was hoped that soon the religion portion of this cooperative program would be accredited so that the full four-year program would be covered by accreditation. Ramsey referred to this arrangement as "a breakthrough, a revolutionary idea." But it was not an idea fully understood or appreciated by many in the church. A "secular" education in a state school was questioned. The recruitment of students remained a struggle. Some students did not have the qualifications for admission to Long Beach State College and most found it very difficult to pay the out-of-state costs for that first year. By 1968 there were fewer students than ten years before. According to the annual publication, *Aletheia,* the 1968 total was only thirty-seven, twenty-seven of whom were from California. Something had to change.

One attempt at fundamental change occurred in 1966 when serious discussions were held with Warner Pacific College about the potential of a merger of the colleges on the site of a gift of land in San Jose, California. Excitement ran high. Warner's board authorized the relocation of its college. But then came a period of questions and indecision, with much unrest related to the feasibility of the move. It finally ended with Warner's board deciding that achieving a sound fiscal operation on the Portland campus was the college's first obligation. President Gough presented his resignation because he judged that his leadership had been eroded seriously. Another possibility for Arlington College had finally died in discussion. So Arlington continued to hope that the Long Beach plan would catch hold and prove fruitful.

In the period just prior to 1968 the stance of the Western Association (official area accreditation body) changed in regard to cooperative endeavors, such as that between Arlington and Long Beach State College. Earlier a program with limited objectives, such as Arlington's religion program, could be accredited in a special category if it were part of a recognized cooperative endeavor and the objectives were being achieved. But by 1968 this special category of accreditation had been dropped, forcing an institution to mount the full four-year program on its own. Arlington just didn't have the resources necessary. All doors seemed to be closed since a cooperative venture was no longer viable and a small, unaccredited college was not adequate for the youth of the church. But in the background another merger possibility was developing, the one possibility that would soon materialize and determine the shape of the future.

In 1967 Dr. Cornelius Haggard, president of Azusa Pacific College in the Los Angeles area, was resource leader at a retreat of Church of God ministers in Southern California. He shared with Arlington's president, Dewayne Bell, board chair, Charles Benson, and board member, Will Denton, about how God had blessed a merger in 1965 of Azusa College and Los Angeles Pacific College. He reported his own tie with the Church of God through the long-term use in his classes of Russell Byrum's *Christian Theology* volume. He issued an invitation for Arlington to consider such a merger with Azusa. The invitation seemed timely, even providential.

At first and for several reasons the Arlington board and area Church of God ministers were hesitant about this merger proposal. For instance, all Church of God faculty members would have to sign a statement of faith, a practice traditionally considered "denominational" in the Church of God. Some wondered about the unknowns of training Church of God leadership in an interdenominational setting, despite the irony of members of a movement committed to Christian unity entertaining such a sectarian concern. But, whatever the cautions, the options were very few, and this particular possibility seemed to present some very promising features. The idea was shared with the Commission on Christian Higher Education of the Church of God which responded with the following in its January 1968 meeting:

> The Commission concurred with President Bell that there appears to be compatible educational concerns and impressive theological affinities with Azusa Pacific. . . . This Commission . . . commends President Bell for the creativity and courage of his Board in appraising the options and recommends this one as worthy of consideration.

Finally, in 1968 the Arlington board voted unanimously to proceed with this merger. On March 4, 1968, this action was ratified by vote of the Association of the Church of God of Southern California. The Long Beach campus was sold with a good profit realized. Some of the proceeds were designated to fund long term a course in Church of God history and doctrine and scholarships for Church of God students at Azusa. Several hundred volumes, including the back issues of the *Gospel Trumpet,* went to the Azusa library with many of the others going to Warner Southern College and Gulf-Coast Bible College. There was some transfer of remaining funds, about fifty thousand dollars, and the establishment at Azusa of an "Arlington Room" as a perpetual memorial. President Bell became assistant to the president at Azusa, both full-time faculty members (Richey and Shackleton) joined the Azusa faculty, and several Arlington board members became part of the Azusa board.

All things considered, a significant Church of God presence went to Azusa as a result of the merger. Arlington finally had found its permanent location, its means of achieving accreditation and a way of providing long-term service to the church.

After years of experience with the results of this merger, reflections and analyses vary. Dewayne Bell has expressed satisfaction at his central role in achieving the merger. "Arlington added to the weight of the Church of God in the Southwest," he said, "and at least some of that valuable reality has been perpetuated through Azusa." Arlington never could have provided such service to the Church of God on its own and under the circumstances that existed at the time of the merger. Charles Benson, board chair of Arlington at the time of the merger with Azusa and still an Azusa board member, has affirmed both that the merger was "a great move forward" and that, even so, the Arlington years were "the peak years of excitement" for the churches in Southern California, unmatched before or since.

In 1976 Paul Sago, a Church of God minister and former vice-president for financial affairs of Anderson College, became president of Azusa. Under his strong leadership Azusa Pacific University has grown in strength and influence in the higher educational community. It has continued to be related, both structurally and programmatically, to the Church of God in Southern California.

A typical analysis of the Arlington experience is that of Maurice

Berquist. A necessary thing (the merger) has become a good thing. While Azusa "salvaged much of what we had hoped to do through Arlington," he said, he also added with some sadness that Arlington on its own might have been such a school if a few circumstances had been different. Arlington was a worthy venture, but it suffered the untimely loss of Herb Joiner. Finally the dollars, students, and church support just were not adequate.

Milo Chapman, longtime leader of Warner Pacific College (PBC) and faculty member at Arlington from 1964-1967, has expressed some disappointment, feeling that Church of God efforts on the West Coast would have been served better if the earlier merger talks with Pacific Bible College had proven successful. There is good reason for a church body to maintain its own higher education, he felt. He concluded with the judgment that the Church of God has enjoyed only modest control or visibility at Azusa, with a continuing confusion in the minds of many about whether it is "our school." But George Ramsey judged the merger with Azusa a "very fine liaison with kindred denominations." Fred Shackleton, longtime dean of Arlington and now chair of Azusa's Department of Religion and Philosophy, not sure that control should be the issue, stated that this multidenominational model of Christian higher education is actually a fine expression of what the Church of God has always said it believed in. And Azusa's current Church of God president, Paul Sago, has said that, "if control is an issue to be discussed, it should be pointed out that no church controls Azusa Pacific."

Arlington College has become a part of what now is Azusa Pacific University. For Arlington, in one sense, that merged identity represents a dream that died of practical necessity. In another sense the dream goes on in a larger way than originally thought possible.

Notes

Beyond all documents referred to in the text, the above chapter drew upon information available through taped interviews or personal letters as follows:

Dewayne Bell, January 16, 1980 and March 6, 1985.

Charles Benson, September 18, 1985.
Maurice Berquist, December 5, 1979.
Milo Chapman, February 25, 1980.
Eugene Conover, April 7, 1980.
Wilford Denton, April 17, 1985 (letter).
Gerald Marvel, May 17, 1980.
Norman Patton, April 23, 1985.
George Ramsey, November 7, 1979.
Herschell Rice, April 14, 1980.
Everett Richey, November 20, 1985 (letter).
Paul Sago, September 25, 1985 (letter).
Fred Shackleton, May 12, 1980.

Table 4
Arlington College
(Azusa, California—as now merged)

Institutional Names:
   1954-1968 Arlington College
      Initially operated during 1953-1954 primarily as a lay academy under the successive names: Southern California School of the Bible, California Christian College, and World Evangelism Institute. Located in Arlington, California, from 1954-1960, then in Long Beach, California, from 1960 until the merger in 1968 with Azusa Pacific College in Azusa, California.
   1968-1981 Azusa Pacific College (merger)
   1981-   Azusa Pacific University (merger)

Accreditations:
   1954-1968 Not accredited
   1968-   Joint with Azusa Pacific University

Chief Executive Officers:
   1954-1955 Maurice Berquist
   1955-1960 C. Herbert Joiner, Jr.
   1960-1961 Earl L. Martin (acting)
   1961-1963 George H. Ramsey
   1963-1968 Dewayne B. Bell
   1968-1975 Cornelius Haggard (Azusa merger)
   1975-1976 An Administrative Team (Azusa merger)
   1976-   Paul E. Sago (Azusa merger)

Chief Academic Officers:
   1954-1956 Albert J. Kempin
   1956-1968 Frederick G. Shackleton
   1968-   Joint with Azusa Pacific University

Current Chair of Governing Board:
   1968-   Joint with Azusa Pacific University

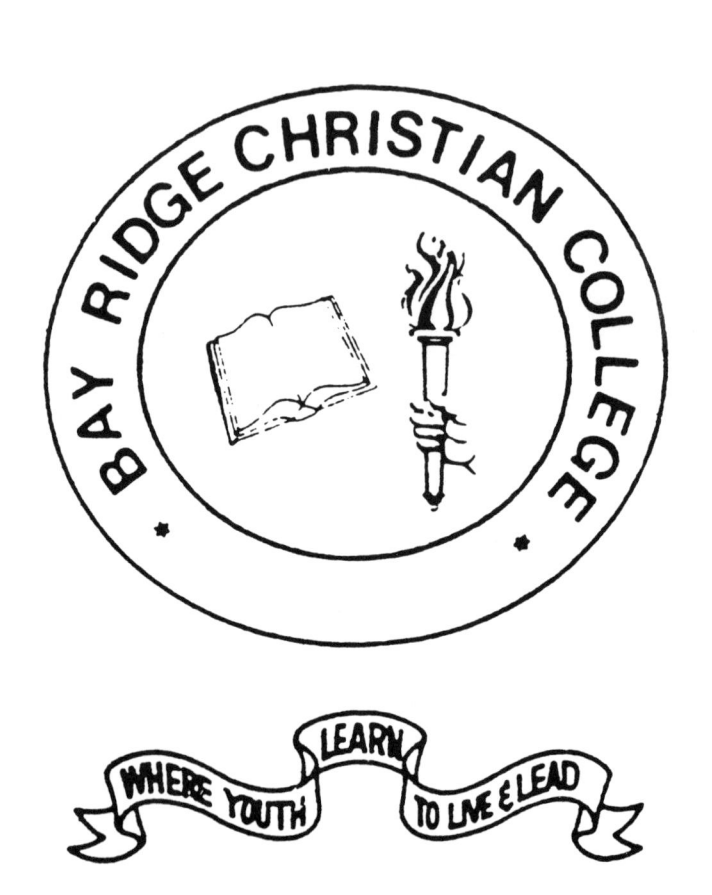

BAY RIDGE CHRISTIAN COLLEGE

WHERE YOUTH LEARN TO LIVE & LEAD

Chapter 5
The Story of Bay Ridge Christian College

Daniel S. Warner demonstrated in his ministry one reason why the Church of God reformation movement has had unusual success in carrying on a productive ministry to Black persons in the United States. In 1890 he engaged in an evangelistic tour in Mississippi and became the victim of an angry mob. The anger came, in part, because Warner showed no discrimination toward Black persons in his public meetings or his visitation of the sick. While recuperating from personal injuries in a cabin outside Union, Mississippi, he wrote the words to the hymn "Who Will Suffer With the Saviour?" To be true to the implications of the Christian gospel will bring opposition from the world.

Rev. Mack Caldwell became an early pioneer in attempting some training effort for Black leaders in the Church of God. He moved to Augusta, Georgia, in 1925 to direct a small educational effort known as Southern Bible Institute. There was an adequate facility there which housed an annual camp meeting for the area Black church. Caldwell directed the institute as a branch of Anderson College (University), receiving some funding from the College and drawing heavily on the theology teaching outlines of Anderson's professor Russell R. Byrum. This institute was a sacrificial effort to assist with the needs of the "colored" people. It existed for two years, served about fifteen students, and then closed because of lack of adequate finances. But it had been a beginning.

In 1937 along the very rural road in Mississippi which ran close by where Warner earlier had been nurtured back to health after the mob violence nearly fifty years earlier, a young, white farm boy dedicated his life to whatever God had for him. J. Horace Germany did not know then that his later ministry would focus on the particular needs of Black persons and, like Warner, it also would nearly cost him his life at the hands of an angry Mississippi mob.

Horace Germany's commitment to Christian ministry led him to Anderson College in 1937. It was there in a sociology class taught by Leona Nelson that he did research and wrote a paper on "The Negro Educational Problem in the South." He came to feel very uncomfortable because of the magnitude of the problem. He noted that there was not one college graduate in the 228 little Church of God Black congregations in the South. There was ignorance of the problem among Whites and there existed the status quo of segregated ministerial assemblies. He felt "thoroughly condemned" about how little the church was doing to help.

Blacks were not permitted to go to White schools in the South in those years. A few did come North, like Isom Crockett and a few others at Anderson College, but only a few and often they didn't return home. So Germany concluded that what was needed was a new school in the South designed for the particular needs of young Black church leaders. He now was a young Christian man with a sensitive social conscience and a cause to bring focus to his own life and ministry.

In 1944, having completed the Bachelor of Theology degree at Anderson College, Germany returned to pastor his home church near Union, Mississippi. He built a new building out of blocks made by hand, modeled after the Old Main building at Anderson College. In 1948 he returned north to Muncie, Indiana, to pastor a congregation near Ball State University. There he started one of the first university student fellowships in the Church of God. He continued to build acquaintances with Black students at nearby Anderson College, learning that he could have "good fellowship" with men like Isom Crockett and Emery Williams despite the racial and cultural differences.

Germany shared among his Black friends his idea of an integrated, Church of God sponsored school for Blacks in the South, but he met some skepticism. They had not often worked quite that way with White persons before. It was an idea not commonly accepted in the South, although there were colleges for Blacks with vocational orientation such as Germany envisioned. But Germany persisted. He began attending the New Orleans Institute and became a friend of the host pastor, George W. Burns, and many other Black ministers who heard and appreciated his vision and courage.

This institute had been operating since the mid-1940s as an annual two-week training experience for Black pastors. The idea had been conceived by A. T. Rowe of the Gospel Trumpet Company. It had been operated for several years with financial support from the company and the Women of the Church of God, organizational direction from T. Franklin Miller of the national Board of Christian Education, and instructional support from many persons in the Anderson church agencies and elsewhere. Included was Charlie Cheeks from Laurel, Mississippi, who had become burdened for the fair treatment and training of Blacks when he visited Caldwell's Southern Bible Institute in the 1920s.

While still pastoring in Muncie, Indiana, Germany began building a dairy cattle herd in Mississippi. Various persons from Anderson College started a project among themselves and helped buy one of the first cows. By 1952 he had moved back to Mississippi to work toward the fulfillment of his dream. With the help of a $10,000 loan from the Board of Church Extension and Home Missions he bought sixty acres of ground south of Union, near Decatur, built a barn, and began a small dairy operation that he hoped would allow Black students without money to earn their education and develop work skills necessary for a tent-making ministry in the South (model of the Apostle Paul). He also spread the word in places like the New Orleans Institute that his intention was to start a college for the church by offering classes scheduled around the working demands of the farm. He believed that long-term leadership development was vital for the Black churches of the South. These leaders must be trained to be self-sufficient and responsible, breaking the welfare cycle by allowing them to work for their education. It must not be a school *for* Blacks (another White handout), but a venture *with* Blacks (there has always been a majority of Black persons on the governing board of the school which evolved). While later history would raise questions about whether this method of approaching the problem was viable and adequate, certainly the cause was right, Germany saw no other way to go, and his commitment to it was complete.

The Board of Church Extension and Home Missions in Anderson had interest in opening a work among Blacks in the South. In 1952 Isom and Ola Crockett were added to the staff of the Board for work in Mississippi. The Crocketts, James Stewart, Harold Chesterman, and Horace Germany formed a ministry team for the state. But Germany's dream was a school. In March 1954 the first session of a planning committee for a training school met in Decatur, Mississippi. It considered how a Board of Trustees should be formed. Isom Crockett acted as group secretary. Additional acreage was secured across the highway from the original land for a "manual training school."

A tentative organizational plan for guiding the school project was agreed to by the Board of Church Extension and Home Missions, involving a committee on planning and operation. The committee consisted of Germany, four members from each of the White and Black state church constituencies, and two officers of the Board. William E. Reed of the Board made numerous trips to Mississippi in the years that were to follow. Isom Crockett recalls that the new school was patterned somewhat after Piney Woods Country Life School near Jackson, Mississippi. Germany had studied the goals and operation of the School of the Ozarks in Missouri and Berea College in Kentucky. Students could work at a trade to help pay their bills.

Financial problems soon plagued the project. Interest payments became delinquent on the loans made by the Board. In 1956 ten acres of the total land involved was deeded to the Board as a way of beginning to address the delinquency. At about the same time local opposition began to build against the idea of a college for Blacks. The Germany family decided that the local resistance and the limited acreage for cattle were obstacles too great for the success of the school. In 1957 they bought 140 acres from a relative. This was six miles west of Union, near where Horace had pastored for seven years. By 1959 another 120 acres were purchased and an excellent site for the school had begun to be developed. In March 1960 the original 60 acres which had become deeded to the Board of Church Extension were sold so that the Board's investment could be recovered. Later the additional acreage across the highway also was sold by the Board.

These years of relationship between the Board and the school project directed by Germany had been frustrating and tension-filled for both parties. The finances had been a major problem. A pronounced philosophical difference existed regarding the type of training needed. Germany was committed to a college approach, and the Board questioned the necessity or wisdom of this approach, not having the resources to support such a program. Finally Germany felt abandoned by the Board and the Board felt, because of Germany's decision to leave the farm which the Board had financed, that Germany had separated himself from the administrative guidance of the Board.

The Board felt this estrangement even further when a separate corporation was set up to operate the school. Germany continued to believe that the Board lacked real commitment to the project and had backed off in the face of pressure from southern White ministers. But the Board insisted that to call the venture a college was misleading to prospective students and was promising more than could be delivered. It suggested rather that the focus should be on the original concept of a "manual training school."

Bay Ridge Christian College was organized in 1959 in a meeting to which all Church of God state chairpersons in the South, Black and White, were invited. Forty-six persons were present to elect Horace Germany president and George Burns vice-president. The first students were enrolled in January 1960, with Isom Crockett elected as dean and James Stewart secretary-treasurer. Earlier, persons like Dr. Val Clear and Dr. Louis Gough from Anderson College had served voluntarily on an advisory committee and had assisted in the development of the first curriculum design and catalog.

The Commission on Christian Higher Education of the Church of God had been approached by the college for guidance and recognition, but it had seen the project as a home mission venture, not a college. Since the Board of Church Extension and Home Missions did not support the college emphasis and then had become separated formally from the project, the school had to seek such guidance from interested persons until a formal organization could be established. For a time it was a fragile institutional reality with no parent body. Such a body soon was formed in New Orleans during an institute meeting. It was to be known as the Southern Association of the Church of God. But before it was reality a near tragedy occurred.

On June 13, 1960, the Secretary of State of Mississippi informed Bay Ridge Christian College that its application for a charter of incorporation had been denied by the governor. Racial tension was high. In Little Rock, Arkansas, national attention was drawn to the refusal by state officials to allow Blacks to enroll at Central High School. Germany was branded a "Yankee" probably sent in by the federal government to force a confrontation over integration in Mississippi. Governor Ross Barnett sent sheriffs and warnings to Bay Ridge. This integrated activity (a White president and six Black students) was to stop or there would be severe consequences. And there were. On August 21, 1960, in Union, Mississippi, a mob of about thirty white men beat Germany and left him for dead!

With the help of a sympathetic doctor and a Catholic hospital in Meridian, Germany survived. The local KKK then tried to bankrupt the school before Germany was out of the hospital, but a White feedstore man in Union, Ray Richardson, bought the outstanding bank notes and saved the property at the risk of his own life. Since the students were threatened with hanging if they remained, they went to George Burns' church in New Orleans to finish the school term. There they were taught by James Stewart and Isom Crockett while President Germany traveled to generate support for the school.

Some embarrassment was felt in Union. On August 23 these words appeared in the *Delta Democrat Times* of Greenville, Mississippi:

What is wrong with a town or a county in which wanton brutality is tolerated, ignored, or gleefully applauded? What is wrong with a people when they consider it a crime to build a college dedicated to training men, no matter what color, to be preachers of God's word? What is wrong with the moral climate in which this kind of barbarism can be safely perpetrated?

The college's board met in Houston, Texas, where the racial climate was much better. Richardson received payment for the $19,000 of notes he had secured and he personally provided the trucks to move the school's cattle to Texas. Fearing likely reprisals, ministers of the area did not involve themselves openly by offering any assistance.

Although the separation between the school and the Board of Church Extension and Home Missions had occurred prior to these violent events, it was perceived by many, particularly in the Black church community, that the Board had forsaken Germany at the time of his greatest need. There were confrontational meetings in which the Board had to explain and defend its position.

The move from Mississippi made permanent the school's separation from the Board. From the new Texas location Germany began his personal promotion of the school across the church. It now had its own charter from Texas, was governed by its own board of trustees, and had the Southern Association of the Church of God as its parent body. The Crocketts remained in Mississippi and continued to serve the Church of God faithfully, sometimes at the risk of their own lives and property. The Chestermans moved to Florida.

So the school, to be known as Bay Ridge Christian College, began its life over in a rural setting in Texas. About 230 acres of land were purchased near Kendleton, located forty miles southwest of Houston. The property was adequate and would grow in value. Vocational training was developed, including a dairy herd, and print, auto, carpentry, and machine shops. It was a self-help program. In 1967 the farm land and livestock enterprises generated $44,000 of the college's $110,000 budget and furnished milk and meat for staff and student needs. Classes were scheduled as faculty and students could be available. But the operation remained small and struggling. President Germany traveled extensively telling the school's story and seeking funds and students.

In 1965 the college, represented by the Southern Association of the Church of God, contacted the Commission on Christian Higher Education of the Church of God. It wanted a closer association with the commission. But members of the commission were not well informed about the personnel, programs, management, facilities, and other resources of Bay Ridge. In January 1967, therefore, following a request from Bay Ridge for formal membership in the commission, the commission proposed to send a team to gather information and perspective as a way of helping to determine an appropriate response to the request.

The team of James Earl Massey, Robert A. Nicholson, and Hollie W. Sharpe conducted a campus visit at Bay Ridge on May 19-21, 1968. It then formalized a set of observations and recommendations for Bay Ridge. They included the need for clarifying educational objectives, giving much higher priority to the educational program (over the "farm program"), and facing the dilemma of the church being asked to support two colleges so close together (Gulf Coast Bible College was located in nearby Houston).

Germany responded to these observations and recommendations in a document dated May 16, 1969. He defended the necessity of the trade school department and stated an aspiration for academic progress. Some attention was being given to the admittedly inadequate library and the board of Bay Ridge had determined that the college would "work toward becoming an accredited Bible College and an accredited trade school." He argued that the fact that Bay Ridge and GBC were only forty miles apart was not relevant to the potential of the church supporting both. In fact, "BRCC has no overlapping in service or reason for existence with the GBC program. . . . BRCC has a specific purpose not touched by GBC."

Disagreeing with the team's assertion that BRCC "is by and large a vocational college," Germany insisted that "our major emphases are in the fields of religion and communications, equipping the students for the gospel ministry with enough vocational training to aid them in carrying out this ministry." He asserted that the Church of God was failing in its responsibility to serve the real and very practical needs of southern Blacks. His question was: "Could our general agencies, then, not join in promoting a program which is already in existence (BRCC)?"

This criticism of the church's institutions and the related call for church-wide recognition and support of Bay Ridge were to receive considerable attention in the next few years. Through the Southern Association of the Church of God, Bay Ridge formally requested "general agency" status and thus an annual share in the national World Service budget. The 1975 General Assembly of the Church of God referred this request to the Commission on Christian Higher Education. Considered in the broader context of determining the best way to train Black leaders for service to the church in the South (by direction of the Assembly), more study of Bay Ridge was done by the commission, several Black consultants were brought in from across the country and some thirty Black congregations in the South were visited as one way of assessing the nature and extent of the need.

The result was that in June 1977 the commission reported to the General Assembly its judgment that "the need is urgent, complex in nature, and national in scope, necessitating an approach other than the recommendation of general agency status for Bay Ridge Christian College." Instead of highlighting Bay Ridge as the primary answer, a Black Ministerial Education Fund was established. It was raised each year until being discontinued in 1981. The money was divided among the academic development needs of Bay Ridge, scholarships for eligible Black ministerial students to attend Church of God colleges, and an in-service training program designed by the Center for Pastoral Studies of Anderson School of Theology primarily for Black church leaders with limited education. When the fund ended, the commission was given the continuing assignment of identifying and addressing "the gaps and shortcomings" of several national programs of Black ministerial education, and donors to Bay Ridge were given the privilege of World Service credit for gifts to Bay Ridge channeled through World Service.

Bay Ridge was again urged by the commission to explore with nearby Gulf Coast Bible College "the possibilities of joint programming and other mutual uses of the available human and material resources." After a few modest attempts at such exploration, this effort was dropped. The personalities and differing philosophies and objectives of these schools, as well as the forty miles, kept them quite far apart. In 1985 Gulf Coast moved to Oklahoma City and that move ended the possibility of any cooperative effort.

Another crisis time for Bay Ridge came in the early 1980s. President Germany was talking of retirement. A search was conducted for a successor, with some persons hoping that a Black leader would emerge and accept the presidency. But that hope was not realized. Black persons with the necessary qualifications either were not considered for some reason or seemed not to share the vision of Bay Ridge as the way to meet the needs of the next generations of young Blacks. So Charles Denniston, a young, White construction supervisor who had been with Bay Ridge since 1970 and had earned a degree from it, became president in 1982. He felt unprepared for the task and was aware of the criticism, even cynicism, about Bay Ridge in some quarters. But he was committed to the task and determined to serve in a sacrificial manner. At the conclusion of his five-year term in 1987 Denniston expressed willingness to step aside if appropriate Black leadership became available. And, in fact, that is what the future held.

In 1987 the Board of Trustees of Bay Ridge and the Southern Association of the Church of God announced the election of Dr. Robert C. Williams as the new president of the college, succeeding Charles Denniston, who was to remain as faculty member and director of development. This move to a Black chief executive officer with significant educational credentials and experience was intended to be a positive and aggressive step toward making long-standing hopes more viable in the future.

President Williams announced soon after his election a new "commitment to excellence." He declared that "we can build an institution of Christian higher education . . . looked upon as one of the finest Black colleges in the nation." To do this he envisioned a new drive toward accreditation and the establishment of a more secure financial base accomplished in part by one thousand congregations giving regularly to the college through their local budgets. It was a bold hope in the face of significant odds; but to this school significant odds were nothing new. What was new was fresh enthusiasm and leadership determined to find a way to move hope in the direction of reality.

A 1987 brochure of the college reported that, among more than 13 million Black citizens in eleven Southern states, the Church of God had 187 churches, 58 of which were without pastors. There were 7 million young persons in the region in need of Christian training. This was a large part of the need that Bay Ridge heard calling it forward. So President Williams brought experienced educator Dr. Walter Doty as the new dean. Soon the academic programs had undergone extensive review, a significantly revised catalog was published, and applicant status was achieved with the American Association of Bible Colleges. A more sturdy foundation was beginning to be built for the future.

Bay Ridge always has been small, has struggled for operating resources, and has depended heavily on the vision and personal sacrifice of relatively few persons. Nonetheless, past and present school leaders like Horace Germany and Robert Williams would point proudly to many churches in the South and elsewhere, both rural and urban, now being pastored by Bay Ridge graduates. They would recount with satisfaction the names of faculty members who have served without salary and a series of former Bay Ridge students who have gone on to Anderson School of Theology and other graduate schools and have been successful. Although the numbers of such persons are small, college leaders would suggest that, when compared with the success levels of the other of the church's colleges in preparing and placing Black church leadership, the success of Bay Ridge has been remarkable.

Table 5

Bay Ridge Christian College (Kendleton, Texas)

Institutional Names:
  1959-Bay Ridge Christian College
        In 1960 moved from Union, Mississippi, to Kendleton, Texas.

Accreditations:
  Not accredited.

Chief Executive Officers:
  1959-1982 J. Horace Germany
  1982-1987 Charles G. Denniston
  1987-   Robert C. Williams

Chief Academic Officers:
  1959-1960 Isom R. Crockett
  1960-1970 John A. Buehler
  1970-1971 J. Horace Germany (while president)
  1971-1974 Raymond E. Hastings
  1974-1975 Sawak Sarju
  1975-1976 J. Horace Germany (while president)
  1976-1977 Charles G. Denniston
  1977-1987 Elbert Williams
  1987-   Walter M. Doty

Current Chair of Governing Board:
  1985-   Preston Ervin

Chapter 6
The Story of Gardner Bible College

Harry C. Gardner graduated in 1924 from Anderson Bible Training School and Seminary in Anderson, Indiana. He returned to his native Canada and soon became the respected pastor of the Church of God congregation in Edmonton, Alberta. But now he had a particular focus of concern that went beyond his pastoral responsibilities. It was a burden to establish in the Canadian setting a Christian training program something like what he himself had profited from in Anderson. The college that finally would evolve from this burden, although never large, would prove to be pivotal in the development of much of the general work of the Church of God in Western Canada in the decades to follow.

Fulfilling such a dream, however, would have to occur in the midst of the prevailing realities of the Church of God on the Western Canadian prairies in those years. Those realities included relative newness as a church movement, pronounced ethnic and language diversities among the people, and the lack of organizational development within the church. It also was a time of widespread financial hardship that soon would grow even worse. The need for Christian training, in short, was far more evident than were the ways and means of meeting it.

For several years the possibility of a new school was discussed among the area ministers, with action always being postponed

Gardner Bible College

until circumstances became more favorable. But the concern persisted because trained leadership was lacking and many of the church's young people were being lost from the life of the Church of God. It was difficult and expensive for most Canadian young people to go as far away as Anderson in the mid-western United States for the necessary training. Some had been choosing to attend an interdenominational Bible school near Edmonton. These persons, however, often were drawn away from the Church of God by the new relationships made and opportunities encountered.

Finally, in a minister's meeting in Lashburn, Saskatchewan, in 1932, Gardner shared persuasively his vision and burden for starting a Bible school in Edmonton. His sharing inspired agreement that this proposed school project had potential and deserved encouragement and support. The ministers passed a brief resolution authorizing the establishment of a training school. Initial implementation was left to Gardner's best judgment and efforts. It was a time of severe depression economically and determined hope spiritually. Considerable dedication and sacrifice would be required.

There were only a few well-established congregations of the Church of God in Western Canada, although there were many more saints living in isolated communities and reading the *Gospel Trumpet* or the *Evangeliums Posaune.* Probably there were some six hundred Church of God persons in all, about half German-speaking, a few Ukrainian and Russian, and the rest English.

One Church of God woman, Sarah Monroe, responded to the difficulties of the times by moving with her husband to Edmonton to start the Mission of the Open Door as a way of helping some of the hardest hit people in the heart of the city. The hungry, mostly unemployed men, were fed with donated food supplies. A meal was served at the mission each evening after a gospel service conducted by Rev. Gardner and others whom he supervised. In this mission, on January 3, 1933, with eleven students enrolled in classes, the school began. Students lived with local Church of God families. "Mother" Monroe, H. C. Gardner, and Walker Wright, also a graduate of Anderson Bible Training School, were the teaching staff. Gardner directed the small enterprise, a long dream beginning to materialize, if only in a modest way.

Those first students soon were expressing deep gratitude for the supportive atmosphere and the learning opportunity. They wanted their lives to count for God and the work of his kingdom. So a good report of that first term reached the Ministers and Workers Assembly at the Church of God camp meeting in Ferintosh in July, 1933. Apparently, such a training institution was indeed viable despite all of the problems. Persons were chosen to promote the school and guide its development. The school already had moved from a prayerful dream to a functioning reality. Gardner had put out the challenge for support in these words: "Let us pray and work for a bigger and better School next winter. Do not forget the Bible School in your future plans. If you cannot come perhaps you can raise a few extra chickens, feed a calf or a pig, grow some extra vegetables, sow a few acres of wheat, or do something to help the School next winter" (*Canadian Messenger,* April 1933, p. 3).

The next winter term (January-March 1934) found the school operating with thirteen students in the basement of the Edmonton church and with thirty-three more students in a German school in Medicine Hat under the direction of Jacob Wiens, bilingual pastor of the German congregation there. By that summer the school, now known as Alberta Bible Institute, solved the problems of two locations and poor facilities by merging the two operations into one at Ferintosh where Victor and Elsie Lindgren were host pastors and where the large camp meeting tabernacle was located. These two language groups in the church worked together smoothly as this joint venture of faith proceeded. Instruction was to be in English, but a German language class was provided whenever it was needed.

In 1935 an old hospital building became available in Camrose, Alberta. So the decision was made for the institute to move one more time, this time to a location which was to be its long-term home. Wiens moved to Camrose as vice-principal. He and Principal Gardner determined that together they would build the school.

Although 1936-1938 were severe years of economic depression, ABI flourished, reaching an enrollment of sixty students and sponsoring the "ABI Gospel Hour" radio program. Camrose, in the Province of Alberta, was becoming the focal point of the work of the Church of God in Western Canada. The Ferintosh tabernacle was dismantled and moved the thirty miles to Camrose. Publication of the *Western Canadian Contact* also was based in Camrose. When the first issue appeared under the new name of *The Gospel Contact* in October 1942, ABI was its featured subject. By then it was clear that the school had become an important part of the life of the approximately thirty-five Church of God congregations in Western Canada, over half of these in the Province of Alberta.

Real trouble, however, soon came over the horizon. There was war in Europe. Some Church of God young men became active in the Canadian military. Feelings in the country intensified against German people and, in spite of efforts to avoid it, some strain developed in German-English relationships within the Church of God in Canada. After the war a large number of refugees from Europe came to Canada, including many displaced Germans. Among them in 1949 was Gustav Sonnenberg, a widely-known Church of God leader in Europe, his family, and many others who had known and respected him in their former homeland. He became pastor in Wetaskiwin, drew many of the newcomers, and traveled widely as a successful evangelist. He then moved to Edmonton to pastor a German congregation which became the largest Church of God congregation in Canada.

In the midst of this social tension and change after World War II, ABI continued to develop and play a vital role in the Western Canadian church, including being a means of positive communication and fellowship between the English and German church leaders. The Legislative Assembly of the Province of Alberta granted to ABI an act of incorporation in 1947 with the church's General Ministerial Assembly being empowered to elect the school's nine-member Board of Trustees. The college's stated purpose was "the providing of intellectual and spiritual training for prospective ministers, missionaries, and gospel workers and of promoting the true principles and teachings of the Bible as taught and exemplified by Jesus Christ."

In 1949 a high school was established in connection with ABI by the Ministerial Assembly. It was under the leadership of Wilhelm and Irene Ewert and in part had developed out of a concern about the educational level of many ministers who had not completed high school. Even though this new educational project was accredited by the Department of Education of the province, which certainly increased the public stature of ABI itself at the time, library and laboratory resources and enrollment levels were just not adequate to justify continuance. By 1957 the high school was discontinued, as the radio program had been in 1956.

By 1950 ABI's President Gardner was facing a series of problems, including some criticism of his own leadership of the school. He decided to contact a young American minister, Kenneth Jones, to see if he would consider coming to Canada as the first formal dean of the school. Jones, a graduate of Anderson College and Oberlin Seminary, was then in Princeton, New Jersey, doing further graduate work. He had felt a divine call to a teaching ministry and so decided to accept the ABI opportunity and challenge. When he arrived he found ABI going through difficult times. Gardner soon left the school, partly in response to criticism of his own leadership and partly for reasons that, according to Jones, kept his own service limited to only one year.

The lack of educational resources and low student enrollment were not the only problems. Some continuing tension was rooted in a conflict commonly experienced by a dedicated immigrant community seeking to retain the integrity of its own traditions. Rev. Sonnenberg, for instance, was very concerned that the introduction of the English language into the German church in Canada would bring cultural decay and religious compromise, particularly to the new generation of German young people. Only the German language, therefore, was judged appropriate for public preaching and praying. The German Christians formed their own church organization, held occasional Bible classes in Sonnenberg's congregation beginning in 1956, and actually formalized their own Bible school in 1964.

These concerns and developments inevitably came to involve ABI and sometimes the results tended to be divisive even though efforts were made at understanding and reconciliation. Jones returned to the United States to pastor, Gardner ended his long tenure of leadership, and Gordon Schieck attempted to bring some new stability to the institution and to help it be a positive force in the life of the church. But student enrollments, always small, declined during the 1950s. Church support was not adequate and, at times, not even enthusiastic.

Gordon Schieck, wanting missions experience and hoping then to bring that thrust back to enrich the ministry of the school, left for India in 1955. Thomas Hall served as president from 1955-1957. Then, in an especially difficult period for the school, Gardner was called upon to return to the presidency of ABI. He served again from 1957 until his sudden death in 1961. His years of service had been many and they had included challenges and frustrations as well as the joys of leadership training for the church. It had been "his school" for many years. Now his death and the growing educational demands of the times were to issue in a new era.

Whatever the persistent problems, there continued to be quality persons of real dedication associated with the school, persons who had vision and stimulated program development despite the problems. Harry Dodge became dean in 1953 and soon the four-year Bachelor of Theology degree program was initiated. Dean Olt of Anderson College visited during 1953-54 to assist in establishing the necessary new courses. Douglas Welch, later a long-term missionary in East Africa and then professor of Christian mission at Anderson School of Theology, was one of the first students to enter this expanded program.

Richard Yamabe, a graduate of the University of British Columbia and Anderson School of Theology, continued the upgrading of the program through his teaching and academic administration over a period of almost twenty years. This tradition was carried on by others, particularly Siegfried Belter, educated at ABI and the University of Alberta and an excellent bridge person to the German church. Belter was a strong academic person who worked tirelessly to strengthen the educational life of the school. At Belter's untimely death in 1984, John Howard, the current dean who was educated at Anderson College, its School of Theology and the University of Winnipeg, came to carry on this tradition.

Over these years the college worked as it could at strengthening academic programs despite severe economic restrictions. It kept in touch with the larger higher education community through its affiliation with the Association of Canadian Bible Colleges and the Commission on Christian Higher Education of the Church of God.

The 1960s continued to be difficult years for ABI. The school made a series of efforts to develop options and set new and clearer directions. It requested assistance from the Commission on Christian Higher Education of the Church of God. After the Commission's Milo Chapman and Robert Nicholson had visited the campus, it recommended that the Church of God in Western Canada should outline clearly its objectives so that ABI could then align its efforts with them.

In 1968 an important relationship began with neighboring Camrose Lutheran College and consideration was given to an amalgamation of ABI, Mountain View Bible College (Missionary Church), Hillcrest Christian College (Evangelical Church), and Aldersgate College (Free Methodist Church). In 1971 an extensive study was undertaken with the leadership of former ABI student and skilled researcher John Wesley Hughes. Hughes and Schieck made visits to Canadian congregations and colleges. Concurrence was given to the earlier commission recommendation. Calls were also made for the school to remain in Camrose and to develop one- and two-year programs which could be the foundation for continuing studies at Anderson and Warner Pacific Colleges or elsewhere.

Beginning in 1972 some new optimism began to build. An aggressive development program for the school had been launched. David Davis, having graduated from Anderson School of Theology and pastored in Canada, became president of ABI in 1974. Ralph Farmer was in place as director of development. A prime piece of land in Camrose became available and was seen by some as an excellent opportunity for the school to relocate and expand. Planning began toward the possibility of new construction so that the school, the Western Canadian camp meeting, and offices for the national work of the Church of God in Canada could be housed in a conveniently designed and common complex. This would symbolize and help to bring to increasing reality the essential interdependence of these several church organizations—and ABI would be appropriately and closely related to all of the work. But what might have been a giant step forward brought instead turmoil and eventually the resignations of both Davis and Farmer.

Another possible site near Edmonton had become an alternate possibility. It was both attractive and expensive. To some, including Farmer, it seemed almost too good to be true, well worth the risks and major costs involved. To others, including President

Davis, it appeared to be an unwise idea that tantalized some egos but would in fact turn out to be a practical disaster. Sides developed and positions hardened. The resignations followed. Both sites were eliminated, one by the city of Camrose for safety reasons (old coal mines under the property) and the other by lack of the funds necessary for ABI to act in time to secure it. Gordon Schieck again was asked to fill the sudden leadership vacuum and try to carry on in the same location and facilities and in the midst of many strained relationships. There now were very few students and even some talk that it might be necessary to close the school altogether. But that was not allowed to happen.

The pattern for many years had been one of determination mixed with discouragement for ABI. Then in 1977 another era of renewed hope began. Rev. Robert Hazen from Lansing, Michigan, accepted the school's presidency. He had been a member of its governing board, knew its problems, but was nonetheless optimistic about the potential that could yet be its future. So some new plans were drawn for long-term development. Hazen knew that his task was to try to salvage the situation and at least a few things gave him the necessary hope to proceed. There was some strong lay leadership in the church and on the ABI board. Alberta was a rapidly developing area with a strong economic base. The students who did come to the school tended to be persons with talent, drive, and a willingness to adapt and work hard (they often came from immigrant families). Finally, in Hazen's view, the school was needed if the Church of God in Western Canada was to have identity and cohesion. Otherwise that church probably would deteriorate into a scattered collection of essentially community churches.

The years since 1977 have been guided by a series of goals that have been achieved in varying degrees. President Hazen has identified these goal areas as follows:

1. To bring to the Church of God movement at large the unique benefits of "the German theological mind." The coming to the faculty of Anderson School of Theology in 1980 of Dr. Walter Froese from the faculty of ABI is an example.

2. To help the Canadian church capitalize on opportunities not available to the church in the United States or not addressed by the American church. The relatively neutral posture of the Canadian government on the international scene opens some unique

mission opportunities.

3. To be a unifying force in the Canadian church. The very large distances within the country as well as Anglo-German and other divisions have created a real need for such a force. There have been attempts and progress toward ending the polarizations among the college, the Canadian Board of Missions, and the local churches.

4. To establish a sense of continuity and longevity in the school by ending the frequent administrative and faculty changes which had been endured in previous years. The leaving of Dr. Froese and the death of Dean Belter have worked against this goal, but Hazen's own long-term commitment and that of the new dean, John Howard, are positive events.

5. To bring improvement in the aged and inadequate facilities of the college. In fact, two new student dorms and a music hall have been added, and now the offices of the Executive Council of the General Assembly of the Church of God are on the edge of the Gardner campus. This brings increased unification of the school and the ministry agencies of the church in the region.

6. To enhance a significant relationship with the nearby Camrose Lutheran College which had been evolving over the years. This is being accomplished so that Gardner students have convenient access to a range of liberal arts courses. CLC has managed to gain degree-granting status through the Private College Accreditation Board of the Province of Alberta. Gardner is able to grant theological degrees without such accreditation. It relies, then, on the availability of the wider range of CLC courses, a practical way to approach the hope of a quality program with limited financial resources.

In 1980 the name of the school was changed to Gardner Bible College in honor of its founding president. Then, in June 1983 the General Assembly of the Church of God meeting in Anderson, Indiana, joined with Gardner Bible College in celebrating its fiftieth year of service to the Church of God. The college was recognized as the second oldest institution of higher education in the Church of God in North America (only Anderson University is older) and one that had played a significant role in the life of the church. Gordon Schieck earlier had reported through the pages of *Vital Christianity* (July 2, 1978) some of the accomplishments of

Table 6

Gardner Bible College
(Camrose, Alberta, Canada)

Institutional Names:
  1933-1980 Alberta Bible Institute
  1980-   Gardner Bible College

Accreditations:
  Through affiliation with Camrose Lutheran College and Warner Pacific College.

Chief Executive Officers:
  1933-1953 Harry C. Gardner
  1953-1955 Gordon Schieck (acting)
  1955-1957 Thomas M. Hall
  1957-1961 Harry C. Gardner
  1961-1964 J. Milton Chugg
  1964-1966 Albert F. Irving
  1966-1967 Hugh C. Wolkow (interim)
  1967-1974 Gordon Schieck
  1974-1975 David W. Davis
  1975-1977 Gordon Schieck (interim)
  1977-   Robert Hazen

Chief Academic Officers:
  1933-1950 Harry C. Gardner (while president)
  1950-1951 Kenneth E. Jones
  1951-1953 Gordon Schieck
  1953-1957 Harry L. Dodge
  1957-1962 Richard N. Yamabe
  1962-1968 Jarvis C. Wiuff
  1968-1974 Richard N. Yamabe
  1974-1975 David W. Davis (while president)
  1975-1984 Siegfried Belter
  1984-   John Alan Howard

Current Chair of Governing Board:
  1988-   Alexander Ryan

the college over the years. An alumni association had been formed in 1949 and by 1978 there were over seven hundred on the mailing list. Some of these had gone on to excel in additional academic studies at Anderson and Warner Pacific Colleges and elsewhere. Most were active in Christian service as educators, pastors, and leading laypersons. Thirty-two of the Church of God ministers in Canada at the time were Gardner alumni, while others were serving as missionaries in other countries. A wonderful example of missionary service was Irene Engst who served in Kenya from 1947 to 1974.

These numbers have continued to grow. Between 1972 and 1986 there were a total of 163 graduates of Gardner Bible College. Thirty-four of these persons completed the four-year Bachelor of Theology degree. About forty percent of all these graduates are in full-time Christian ministry or are pursuing further studies toward that goal.

Gardner Bible College has never been large in numbers of students, but it has persisted in its prime purposes since 1933. It increasingly has been a pivotal force in the development of much of the general work of the Church of God in Western Canada and through many of its graduates it has provided significant leadership for the church in Canada and worldwide. The college's challenge is substantial as it seeks with limited funding to serve a relatively small and geographically scattered church constituency. That challenge, however, has been faced for decades with persistence and high aspiration.

NOTES

Four published sources that have recorded portions of the history of Gardner Bible College are:

[1] Walter Froese, *Sounding Forth the Gospel on the Prairies* (Gospel Contact Press, 1982).

[2] H. C. Heffren, *Voices of the Pioneers* (n.p., n.d., about 1969).

[3] Daniel Nelms, "A Comparative History of Three Selected Bible Colleges in Alberta," a Ph.D. dissertation, Walden University 1982.

[4] Gordon Schieck, "A Brief History of ABI" in *Vital Christianity* (July 2, 1978).

Chapter 7
The Story of Mid-America Bible College

In one way the origin of Mid-America Bible College stretches as far back as the early 1930s. In that depression period Warner Memorial University was forced to close its doors in Eastland, Texas (see chapter 8). President J. T. Wilson and others who had been associated with Warner Memorial had sensed a need for trained leadership in the church and had begun to build an educational dream. But financial circumstances did not permit that grand dream to survive for long.

While Warner Memorial did not endure, the sense of need for a Church of God college in that part of the country did. By 1950 this hope for an institution of learning had begun to take some shape and potential concreteness again. Concern was expressed in the Midwest Assembly of ministers, and soon the ministerial assemblies of the Church of God in Colorado, Kansas, Nebraska, Oklahoma, and Texas had appointed representatives who together formed a working Board of Directors for a proposed new college. This group, under the leadership of Rev. Max R. Gaulke, pastor in Houston, Texas, since 1947, met in Oklahoma City in 1951 to discuss prayerfully the need and the possibilities.

At this point it was the opinion of the group that a new college,

MID-AMERICA BIBLE COLLEGE • PREPARING EVANGELS OF OUR HERITAGE •

tentatively referred to as Central Bible College, should be founded in either Wichita, Tulsa, or Oklahoma City. Studies of the potential of these locations began. Meanwhile, Rev. Gaulke explored with Frellsen Smith, Church of God layperson and college professor, the possibility of locating the school in Ruston, Louisiana, in relation to Louisiana Tech University. Smith pursued this idea with the university president and State Board of Education, thinking that students of a new church college could take general classes at Tech for credit, enabling the college to concentrate on studies in Bible, theology, and church ministries. Gaulke, however, came to feel that there would be better student employment in a major city setting and the idea of Ruston was dropped. One oil man offered a large gift if Oklahoma City were chosen as the site. But there developed no sense of rightness, no clear view of practical possibility in this or in any of the other options considered.

Gaulke, himself a well educated and sometimes impulsive leader, began to despair of this search process. Someone had to take some action, even if it were only the first step and not eventually the long-term solution. So he took matters into his own hands. As he later wrote, "I was finally pressed by a sense of duty to do something concrete as a start." He initiated plans to open an "institute" in Houston, Texas "as a beginner effort." The board was agreeable to this temporary development while it continued to plan for the founding of a college somewhere in the region. In reality, no other college ever was founded and the Houston institute became the modest base on which the future would be built.

In the spring of 1953, with Gaulke's First Church in Houston planning to host the new institute, Gaulke approached the Texas Ministerial Assembly meeting in San Antonio to seek its support of the educational effort. Some of the ministers were hesitant, fearing another failure like the earlier Warner Memorial University in Eastland, Texas. They certainly didn't want Texas to be known as the graveyard of colleges. But Gaulke assured them that the institute would be a small operation with himself as president and the local congregation in Houston being primarily responsible. So the way was cleared for the modest beginning of South Texas Bible Institute in September, 1953.

Rev. Gerald Erickson, an Anderson College graduate pastoring the Northside Church of God in Houston, was soon convinced by

Gaulke to come full time as dean of the institute. A governing board was constituted, including members chosen by the local church and others selected by the State Ministerial Association of Texas from each of the four Texas districts. Gaulke judged that the institute was on a sound foundation with the Texas State Assembly as its "general legislative body" and with its willingness to be "amenable to the jurisdiction of the General Ministerial Assembly of the Church of God." Erickson, Max and Isabelle Gaulke, and secretary Esther Acheson worked hard to get organized and prepare materials. A recruitment flier was passed out during the 1953 International Convention of the Church of God in Anderson, Indiana, to see, according to Gaulke, "what the Lord would give us by way of students." A small notice appeared in the *Gospel Trumpet* and a letter was read to the General Assembly in June 1953. The way was prepared for a beginning.

When the institute opened its doors in September it owned no property and had a modest budget of $10,000, with only the dean on salary. Twenty-six students had arrived from eight states (Arkansas, Colorado, Kansas, Louisiana, Nebraska, Oklahoma, South Dakota, and Texas). The promised availability of room, board, and work in the city as well as the low tuition rate of thirty-five dollars per semester had proven attractive. The small staff and "pioneer class," as they were called, were dedicated to an educational and evangelistic mission. President Gaulke announced that the institute "was born to such an urgency." Lost men and women would hear the good news "through the activities of trained, spiritual, and zealous followers of Christ." The institute was called to give "intense training" in the Scriptures, personal and mass evangelism, Christian education, and missions. It was hoped that in years ahead such training would develop to the point of being on "a college academic level."

From the institute's beginning there was a degree of tension between it and the national church. On the positive side and according to the first issue of the institute's publication, the *Tidings* (January 1954):

> It wasn't until the brethren in Anderson were notified of our intentions and asked for their criticisms and suggestions that the initial step was taken to organize the school.

A letter from the Acting Secretary of the Commission on Higher Education of the Church of God informed us it was all right to go ahead with our plans.

But there was another side. The general church had just come through some years characterized by strong "anti-Anderson" feelings on the part of some. There had been "watchmen on the wall" who had sat in judgment of certain "headquarters" persons and trends. The remains of that atmosphere were still real. President Gaulke, for instance, didn't always see eye-to-eye with some of his own staff or with general church trends. Critical remarks were made on occasion despite a deep loyalty to the Church of God reformation movement.

Dean Erickson and others opposed vigorously the idea of some who became related to the institute that there be a break with "the Anderson body." Such an idea was never given serious consideration. But a degree of tension persisted. It was partly preoccupation with a perceived regional need; but it went deeper than that. Gaulke was critical of what he judged as the failure of the other colleges to train preachers true to the Church of God. And the general church worried about the financial burden and competition that would result from the existence of another educational institution.

The institute contacted the national Commission on Christian Higher Education to seek dialogue regarding direction and procedures for the new program. President Gaulke, Dean Erickson, and trustees Lloyd Butler and Dr. Loren Rohr then went to Anderson, Indiana, in June of 1954 to meet with the commission. After Gaulke reviewed for the commission the background of the institute's beginning and his own view of the need for such a school, the trustees stated their desire that the venture be critiqued carefully. Does a Bible institute have a legitimate place in the Church of God? They said that they did not wish to support a reactionary or divisive move within the church, one that could not function in harmony with the commission and the General Ministerial Assembly.

There followed some vigorous discussion pro and con about educational philosophy, fundamentalism, and the value of accreditation for a ministerial program. While the commission had no legal jurisdiction, it tried to offer counsel and caution consistent with the ongoing educational efforts of the church. Ironically, in this same June meeting the commission also handled issues related to the World Evangelism Institute in Southern California (later Arlington College), counseling that new training program to be "consistent with the generally accepted philosophy of missionary education in the Church of God."

The life of this little institute gained in strength. In 1954 Walter Doty came from his pastorate in Marion, South Dakota, to teach and, by 1955, to provide academic leadership as dean. He had studied at Anderson College and North American Baptist Seminary in South Dakota and had been burdened for a new school in the South ever since he had been pastor in Ruston, Louisiana (1945-50), and had heard the earliest talk of the possibility.

In the spring of 1955 the trustees voted to expand the curriculum to a four-year Bible college level and change the name to Gulf-Coast Bible College. The Veterans Administration approved the program for veterans. Traveling musical groups were now on the road representing the school in the church. In 1956 the first international students came, including Rolando Bacani of the Philippines, Felipe Merioles of Guam, and Kresten Norholm of Denmark, and the host congregation in Houston erected its educational building, a great boost for the school.

In these early years the possibility still existed that the school's location might be moved. Gaulke and Doty made occasional trips to places like Oklahoma City when offers of land and money came. But nothing firm developed and Houston appeared increasingly to be the college's permanent home.

As the college grew, it continued to deal with the issues of being understood, accepted, and supported by the Church of God at large. President Gaulke (*Tidings,* August 1959) was very clear about the distinctive educational philosophy of Gulf-Coast Bible College. It was specifically a "college of the Bible." There was an important difference between it and a Christian liberal arts college. At GBC every student was required to have a major concentration in biblical studies and do required Christian service as part of the program. The focus was on "training for a life of Christian service." By contrast, according to Gaulke, the Christian liberal arts college provides a liberal arts education under Christian influence with very little Bible or related subjects required of all students. Most students select "secular majors and Christian service is voluntary." The choice for a student, he concluded, is whether to attend "a college of liberal arts which makes available some Bible subjects, or a college of Bible which concentrates in that field but also requires a substantial amount of liberal arts."

The drawing of this sharp contrast between types of schools, when coupled with the assertion that it was obvious which type better prepared Christian leaders and served the church more adequately, brought both students and controversy. Sometimes given congregations became known as GBC or Anderson College or Warner Pacific churches. A longstanding difficulty developed between the School of Theology of Anderson College, the church's only seminary, and some GBC leaders and graduates. Did such graduates need seminary training? If so, given their strong undergraduate Bible background, how could the curriculum of the School of Theology be particularly useful for their needs since it was built on a liberal arts base and its requirements were designed primarily for graduates of such institutions? Answers were given and some curricular accommodation provided by the seminary, but the difficulty persisted, at least in the minds of some.

In February 1958 President Gaulke felt keenly the need of a broader base of support for GBC and wished for a wider acceptance of the college. He wrote to the Commission on Christian Higher Education calling for a national educational budget that would include "all of our colleges on some kind of a family relationship basis." He asked that "*all* of our functioning colleges" be recognized in Church of God periodicals and that, to give "a sense of acceptance," World Service credit be given to churches sending money to Arlington College and Gulf-Coast Bible College. The Texas Ministerial Assembly sent a similar request, as did the GBC Board of Trustees, to the Executive Council of the Church of God in March 1958. The trustees asserted that such moves would enable "a larger spirit of harmony" in the national work and would make it easier for GBC graduates to promote World Service in their churches. It was an attempt to gain recognition, acceptance, and dollars for the college and to make the case that a more official status for the college would contribute to the health of the church's life.

The Executive Council referred these requests to the Commission of Christian Higher Education which, on April 10, 1959, stated its judgment that World Service credit should not be given for funds directed to GBC because GBC was not a World Service agency and had not met the necessary requirements for agency status. Those requirements included General Ministerial Assembly election of members of the governing board and ratification of the chief executive officer of an agency and the assumption that an institution seeking agency status "should be expected to demonstrate wide acceptance and approval by the church and have some history of success in achieving stability and purposes consonant with the policies and program of the other general agencies of the Church of God. . . ." GBC was judged not qualified in these areas.

Time, however, would bring change in this judgment. By 1964 the college had made a full presentation of its program to the commission, which in turn reported to the Executive Council its own perceptions of the college's strengths and weaknesses. Progress definitely had been made, but fundamental weaknesses in facilities, faculty credentials, library holdings, and so forth, were still noted. The college had not yet done a comprehensive self-study or "exposed itself to the systematic view of any accrediting agency." The commission concluded that a "qualitative comparison with other colleges of comparable aspiration is the most appropriate means of evaluation." That meant accreditation by the appropriate body, the American Association of Bible Colleges.

The next four years were to be eventful indeed. The commission and Division of World Service pondered the questions related to World Service credit for funds given to a nonagency college and to the criteria for and implications of the possibility of another agency college. Meantime, GBC worked toward formal accreditation. A self-study developed in 1966 recounted the college's origin, purpose, and curricular development. It reported a fall 1965 enrollment of 143 full-time and 65 part-time students, most of whom were affiliated with the Church of God. There were no doctoral degrees held by the nine full-time faculty members. The several programs offered sought to combine a strong Bible/Theology emphasis with a range of "general education" offerings. The five-year Bachelor of Theology degree was identified as the college's "most important project" since most Church of God ministers did not become seminary graduates and thus required this strong undergraduate program which includes a basic foundation for the ministry." The assumption was put forward that "if GBC continues to merit the confidence of the church-at-large, it may be assumed that some method will be found in future years to undergird the financial structure of the institution."

That assumption was well-founded. In April 1968 GBC received accreditation from the American Association of Bible Colleges. In June of that same year GBC became a general agency of the Church of God by action of the General Assembly and was granted representation on the Executive Council and membership in the Commission on Christian Higher Education. Finally the college had become a formal part of the general church family.

Major milestones had been reached, but a long road yet lay ahead for a small, young college. A real sense of acceptance of the college in the church was still not a reality for many persons. Academic respectability was still questioned widely. Finances still presented a major problem.

Dr. Donald Smith became vice-president for academic affairs in 1970. He was a trained educator who brought an increased professionalism to the faculty and liberal arts emphasis in the curriculum. The achievement of the doctorate by Walter Doty in 1971 was a powerful symbol of personal sacrifice and an institutional commitment to excellence. The purchase in 1973 of thirteen thousand volumes from the library of a closed college was a real step forward. In 1975, an historic year, the college bought property from First Church in Houston, constructed a fine new facility for student housing and saw the retirement of its founding president, Dr. Max Gaulke, after twenty-two years of service. Gaulke had had the vision and the persistence in the early and difficult years. He was known as an excellent pastor and preacher and a man of action. He had served as president until 1967 on a part-time basis without salary, but then accreditation standards required his resignation from the pastorate to be a full-time, salaried president. The college under his leadership had come from being merely a dream and a fragile experiment to an established and accredited agency of the Church of God. Clearly 1975 was the end of the initial era of the college's existence and the beginning of another.

Rev. John Conley, Church of God pastor and member of the Board of Trustees of GBC, became executive vice-president of the college in July 1973. Immediately he was faced with the continuing financial problems of a young school. Bills were pending, salaries were low, and the campus was located in a less-than-ideal area of the city of Houston. But ways were found to do what was necessary to survive. In 1975 Conley became the college's second president. He left the pastorate for this challenge, he said, because he had seen young ministers from limited backgrounds nonetheless doing so much in little churches after having been trained "at struggling little GBC." A stronger college, then, could do so much more!

Eleven years later, in 1986, Conley reported that the keynotes of his administration since 1975 had been: (1) To press faculty to complete advanced degrees; (2) To keep the college in the Church of God (some friends of the college still wanted a separation); (3) To prove to the Church of God "that GBC was worthy of respect"; (4) To strengthen general curricular requirements so that the typical student completes a double major, with Bible/theology already being one (Biola University used consciously as a model); and (5) To achieve regional accreditation to assist the placement of graduates because "many in the church saw a Bible college as substandard education."

AABC accreditation was reaffirmed in 1978. The self-study of 1977 reported sixteen full-time faculty members (five with earned doctorates), and thirteen programs of study leading to the Bachelor of Theology (five-year program) and Bachelors of Arts, Science, and Sacred Music degrees. There were thirty thousand volumes in the library. In 1977-78 there were 314 full-time equivalent students, ninety-five percent with Church of God affiliation. Facilities were improving, particularly with the completion in 1978 of a new administration/library building.

Then in 1979 the college was successful in being the first Bible college to be accredited by the Southern Association of Colleges and Schools, the regional accrediting body. It was hoped that this achievement would bring real respect and advantages for graduates. This process had necessitated a further strengthening of the "general education" requirements. In its 1984 self-study for reaffirmation by the Southern Association, GBC stated about its educational programs:

> Each student is broadly educated in the arts and sciences commensurate with a general education germane to much of American higher education of today. A Christian biblical perspective is maintained in the foundational education of the curricula. All baccalaureate degree programs have a second major in biblical studies as supportive of the major or concentrations selected by the student in fulfillment of vocational and career objectives.

Obviously the college had attracted students with a widening range of career goals and had accommodated its programs to their needs and to generally accepted standards in American higher education. While it appeared increasingly to be a small, church-related liberal arts college, it had avoided being such both in name and in the requirement of a second major in biblical/theological studies.

What had been begun in Houston as a temporary institute, while a permanent location was found for a college in the Southwest region, had remained in its original location for more than three decades and had become that college. But the location was not permanent. In 1983 the Board of Trustees bought thirty-five acres of land in Oklahoma City for a new campus. The reasons were several. Houston was not central to the constituency being served. The campus in Houston was in a bad neighborhood with expansion possibilities limited. And, particularly as President Conley saw it, the college had an opportunity to lose "the Houston connection," perceptions of the college as narrow, substandard, in bad surroundings, little more than the extension of a local congregation.

In the summer of 1985 the college moved its operations to Oklahoma City, occupied brand new facilities designed for its needs, established a relationship with the North Central Association of Colleges and Schools (had left the Southern Association's jurisdiction), and assumed the new name of Mid-America Bible

College. Moving a college is an unusual and difficult task. Doing so in a way that alters accreditation jurisdictions is most unusual. Accomplishing such things and being accepted by North Central with no immediate visitation requirement was a real achievement.

Such a move was not without its considerable problems. Some students and staff remained in Houston for personal reasons. The college dean, Odus Eubanks, left the college in an unpleasant set of circumstances to become president of a new interdenominational college to open in Houston when GBC departed. There was concern that the economy of Oklahoma City might not provide student employment the way Houston did. The acting dean, Kenneth Jones, suffered a heart attack during the transition. Most of all, the college's property in Houston did not sell as expected, creating a major financial crisis for the college.

Nonetheless, morale has been high on campus during these first years in Oklahoma City. Emphasis was placed on student retention as uncertainty remained because of the troublesome failure to sell the old campus property in Houston. Rigorous academic self-examination was undertaken in preparation for reaccreditation visits in 1988. A good foundation had been laid by the sacrificial service of long-term persons like academic leader Walter Doty, librarian Ruth Kirks, trustee Robert Pumpelly, and faculty members Robert and Juanita Adams, Donald Brumfield, William MacDonald, Gene Miller, Nelson Trick, and others. It was a new setting, a new image, a fresh beginning.

Notes

Beyond all documents referred to in the text, the above chapter drew upon information available through taped interviews as follows:

John Conley, January 22, 1986.
Walter Doty, February 2, 1980.
Gerald Erickson, September 25, 1985.
Max Gaulke, May 3, 1985.
Dwight Grubbs, September 27, 1985.
Kenneth Jones, January 25, 1986.
Ruth Kirks, January 22, 1986.
Gene Miller, September 16, 1985.

Table 7

Mid-America Bible College
(Oklahoma City, Oklahoma)

Institutional Names:
   1953-1955 South Texas Bible Institute
   1955-1985 Gulf Coast Bible College
   1985-   Mid-America Bible College
              In 1985 moved from Houston, Texas, to Oklahoma City, Oklahoma.

Accreditations:
   1968-   American Association of Bible Colleges
   1979-1985 Southern Association of Colleges and Schools
   1985-   North Central Association of Colleges and Schools (replacing the Southern Association because of the move to Oklahoma)

Chief Executive Officers:
   1953-1975 Max R. Gaulke
   1975-   John W. Conley

Chief Academic Officers:
   1953-1955 Gerald L. Erickson
   1955-1969 Walter M. Doty
   1969-1970 Gene Miller (acting)
   1970-1973 Donald E. Smith
   1973-1981 Walter M. Doty
   1981-1985 Odus K. Eubanks
   1985-1986 Kenneth E. Jones
   1986-   Melva W. Curtis

Current Chair of Governing Board:
   1984-   Robert J. Pumpelly

INTELLECTUAL

WARNER
MEMORIAL
UNIVERSITY

SOCIAL

PHYSICAL

SPIRITUAL

Chapter 8
The Story of Warner Memorial University

There has been only one institution founded as a "university" within the life of the Church of God. In a real sense it appears to have been the lengthened shadow of one man, Rev. Joseph Turner Wilson—who also was so centrally involved earlier in the founding of Anderson Bible Training School (later Anderson University) in Anderson, Indiana.

This university's life, unfortunately, was characterized by a high aspiration that was strangled by severe financial problems from almost its very beginning. Its story is symbolized well by the experience of young Kenneth Jones who years later would play a significant role in Church of God higher education. As a boy of seven in Oklahoma he already was dreaming of going to college to prepare to be a minister and teacher. He heard talk of a university to be founded in his area by the church. He was excited by this and determined that he would attend. But long before he could complete high school it had been founded, lived its short life, and closed its doors.

Anderson Bible Training School was ten years old in 1927. J. T. Wilson, its founding principal, had resided in Dallas, Texas, since

1924 under assignment from the Church of God's national Board of Church Extension and Home Missions. Having been replaced as general manager of the Gospel Trumpet Company, he now was starting a new congregation. Two 1924 graduates of Anderson Bible Training School, John Batdorf and Dora Gerig (later Mrs. John Batdorf), had joined Wilson as assistants.

Wilson had hopes of a liberal arts institution in the church, and he corresponded with President John Morrison in Anderson about such a broadening of the curriculum of that school. But Anderson was not yet ready for this move (although it did occur in 1929). So Wilson turned his attention to talk in Texas of the possible founding of a new institution. This was beyond his assignment from the Board in Anderson and not part of its intended ministry in the area.

At the annual assembly of the Church of God in Texas, held in Gorman in August 1927, a resolution was passed favoring the establishment of a college of "Class A" rank in the Southwest. J. T. Wilson was appointed promoter of the dream and a member of a small committee to review possible sites for its location. Both John Batdorf and Pearl Bailey, wife of the eventual dean of the new institution, recalled active contact between Wilson and Morrison in Anderson during this time. The founding of a new college apparently was being discouraged by Morrison. Anderson was moving rapidly toward a liberal arts curriculum and there was thought to be no need or adequate resource for another college. But by now personal and regional momentum could not be stopped.

On December 6-8, 1927, the Texas assembly met again, this time deciding definitely that the Church of God in Texas, in cooperation with the church in Louisiana and Oklahoma, would establish a new institution of higher learning in Texas. Soon Eastland, Texas, was chosen as the site, primarily because of a gift of sixty acres of land just outside of town. The school was chartered on December 30, 1927, under the name Warner Memorial University and the first meeting of its board included nine members, five from Texas and two each from Louisiana and Oklahoma. J. T. Wilson was chair of its executive committee and soon was named the university's president. The stated purpose of this new corporation was:

The establishment and maintenance of an institution of learning of University rank, for higher learning, including education in all branches for general diffusion of knowledge, and under Christian influences, with authority to confer all University degrees. The said educational institution is to be forever owned, maintained and controlled by the Texas Ministerial Assembly of the Church of God.

The first classes were held on September 19, 1929, in rented facilities in downtown Eastland while the school's own facilities were being built on its own property just outside of town. Wilson urged the Board of Church Extension and Home Missions in Anderson to extend a $15,000 loan so that the new building could be completed. Finally the loan was made, although with reluctance. Coming events were to include the university's loss of any ability to repay any part of this loan.

The 1929-30 catalog announced proudly that the

. . . curricula of many of the best institutions of our land have been examined and the courses of study outlined in this announcement will be found to be in line with those of the best Class A colleges of the South.

During the first year of operation the university was organized into a School of Music, a College of Science and Liberal Arts, and a Preparatory School. The curriculum included designs for both the Bachelor of Arts and Bachelor of Science degrees, with courses projected in a wide range of fields.

The faculty was heralded as unusually strong and promising for a new and small institution. It was comprised of twelve persons, two holding masters degrees (Paul Breitweiser in music and Frellsen Smith in history). The other persons were: Ernest Bailey, dean; Edgar Barnett, Bible; Nettie Campbell, superintendent of preparatory work; Cressie Nelson, art and violin; John Neuman, mathematics; Harry Reynolds, government and Spanish; Lenora Reynolds, voice; Louis Smith, physical science; Beatrice Smith, English; and Hutchins Ward, economics and physical education. It was a venture of faith, a daring dream, a pioneering work.

Breitweiser, graduate of the Chicago Musical College, had met Wilson when Wilson was speaking at the youth convention at Moody Bible Institute in 1928 where Breitweiser was playing the organ. Arrangements were made for him to become the first "dean of music" in the new Texas school the following year. Ernest Bailey, a University of Minnesota graduate in agriculture, read about the new Texas school in the *Gospel Trumpet* and wrote to Wilson. He and his wife Pearl eventually moved to Texas in 1929 so that he could teach biology and be the dean (even though he had had no previous administrative experience). Harry Reynolds had written to Dr. Wilson in 1928 to ask about the university since both he and his wife were college graduates. They were both granted teaching positions. These and the others came believing in a cause and prepared to make personal sacrifices.

The city of Eastland, population about ten thousand, was proud of the new school and hoped very much for its success. It was a county seat, on a major highway, and had been a prosperous oil town. But the prosperity was mostly in the past. And then, of course, only weeks after the school first opened its doors the great stock market crash of 1929 occurred! From then on things moved from difficult to desperate. There was little student employment. Faculty members gardened, sharing what they had. The Reynolds family was typical. Harry and Lenora supplemented the very small cash income from the school with the milk and butter from their own cow. They raised chickens and had a garden. Congregations in the area helped as they could.

A series of persons later to be prominent in the Church of God came and went as either faculty members or students between 1929 and 1933. Included in the list were Aubrey Forrest, later to be president of Taylor University; Carl Kardatzke, later a long-term, beloved faculty member at Anderson College; Elmer Kardatzke, who was to pursue a long and prominent pastoral career; Irene Smith (Caldwell), who began her long and distinguished teaching career in 1931 at WMU; Lester and Kenneth Crose, brothers who returned with their missionary parents from Beruit, Lebanon, in 1930 to begin college at WMU, Lester later to become a prominent leader in Church of God missions and Kenneth to pursue a distinguished teaching career at Warner Pacific and Anderson Colleges; and Paul Breitweiser who returned to Anderson College for a long career in music education. And there were others who pastored churches and did missionary work.

Whatever the dream, however, and despite many quality persons and much personal sacrifice, 1932-33 was to be the last year. The time was wrong. The dollars needed to survive a depression time just were not there. Money which had been pledged could not be paid. The school had fallen victim to economic circumstances beyond its control. Many persons believed that the need was real and the institution valid if only the time and place had been different.

Some persons, like Lester Crose, went on to graduate from Anderson College where his WMU credits were accepted in transfer. Several others finished at Abelene Christian College and other institutions. Only Lucille Kardatzke ever graduated from Warner Memorial. Many persons had invested in the university and eventually lost part or all of what they had entrusted to this cause. Elver Adcock and Carl Kardatzke used the old Ford truck of Anderson College to retrieve the university's library. The Board of Church Extension and Home Missions received title to the property by buying it for $2,000 at public auction in 1935 after attorneys in Eastland had foreclosed. The Board then sold the school's property and facilities to the Church of God in Texas in 1946. Today the church's Camp Inspiration is on the site.

It was a sad end for an idea that a proud and venturesome man like Rev. J. T. Wilson had believed in so deeply. He truly was a visionary and a promoter. He had worked hard, welcomed progressive ideas, and planned big. In 1931 he still believed the university could make it. In 1933, however, he left his post as president for a pastorate. But even after the school closed he worked to find ways to pay some of the bills in Eastland that had to be left behind. It was a painful process of saving face and maintaining integrity in difficult circumstances.

Harry Reynolds, faculty member who had left in 1932 to complete a graduate degree at Northwestern University, was invited by the Warner trustees to return as president following Wilson's resignation. But such was not to be. The university was unable to continue. Ernest Bailey, dean throughout the school's brief existence, returned to Minnesota to work with the Federal Land Bank, never again to be involved in Church of God higher education. John Batdorf, who traveled for the university through the summer of 1930 and then pastored many of its faculty and students in the Eastland church until 1933, also came back north. He later said, "We enjoyed our time in Texas; we got started in ministry." Harry Reynolds became a businessman and then a teacher for many years in Racine, Wisconsin. He later recalled the Texas years fondly, saying that he and his wife "came away much stronger and better fitted for things ahead."

Warner Memorial University at least got started in its educational ministry, but the start was fragile and short-lived. Attempts to revive it failed and the pain left in its wake was very great for many persons. Not until about twenty years later did serious talk begin again about the need for a college in the Texas/Oklahoma area. That talk eventuated finally in the founding of South Texas Bible Institute in Houston, Texas, in 1953 (later to be Gulf-Coast Bible College and then Mid-America Bible College in Oklahoma City, Oklahoma). This later school was to represent a somewhat different educational vision and philosophy from Warner Memorial, but it was a continuation of the concern to have a Church of God institution of higher education located in that part of the country.

NOTES

Beyond all documents referred to in the text, the above chapter drew upon information available through taped interviews or personal letters as follows:

Elver Adcock, February 24, 1986.
James Bailey, January 5, 1988
Pearl Bailey, March 4, 1980.
John Batdorf, May 5, 1979.
Paul Breitweiser, December 6, 1979.
Lester and Ruthe Crose, January 24, 1980.
Eva-Clare Kardatzke, January 17, 1980.
Harry Reynolds, March 7, 1986.
Frellsen Smith.

Table 8

Warner Memorial University (Eastland, Texas)

Institutional Names:
  1929-1932 Warner Memorial University
  1932-1933 Warner Memorial College

Accreditations:
  Not accredited

Chief Executive Officer:
  1929-1933 Joseph T. Wilson

Chief Academic Officer:
  1929-1933 Ernest O. Bailey

Chair, Governing Board:
  1929-1933 M. B. Boucher

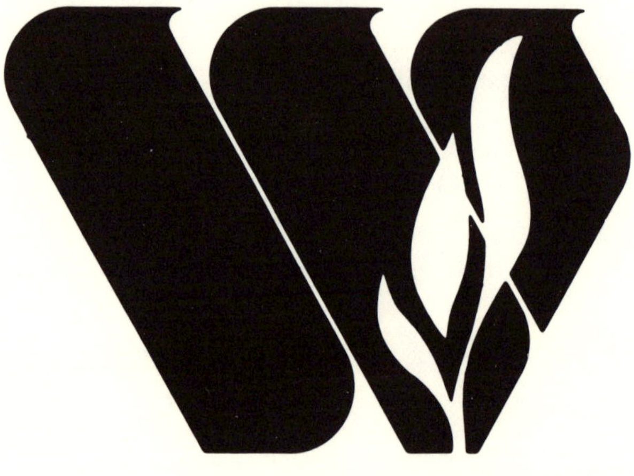

Chapter 9
The Story of Warner Pacific College

Interest in Christian education and ministerial training among Church of God leaders in the Pacific Northwest was evidenced as early as 1905. Formal classes began to be offered in different cities. One educational center which developed was the missionary home in Spokane, Washington, under the guidance of George W. Bailey, a returned missionary from India. These classes soon were supervised by the Inland Empire Ministerial Assembly and were formalized into the Spokane Bible School with Rev. O. A. Burgess as principal from 1916-1918 and G. W. Bailey from 1918-1920. Bailey announced in the *Gospel Trumpet* in 1919 that "the first object of this school is to help those who feel the call to the ministry or some other branch of gospel work, such as teaching God's word. . . . Come expecting to work hard, to be criticized, and to be instructed and encouraged in the divine life."[1]

This educational effort, after being affected negatively by World War I, found two more years of life when it relocated in Boise, Idaho, in October 1920. This city was felt by some to be a more central and advantageous location. Under the new name of Pacific Bible Institute and with Rev. Albert F. Gray as principal, the Northwest Ministerial Assembly became the guiding body. But low enrollment (never reaching thirty students), poor facilities, and lack of adequate student employment caused leaders to move the school again in 1922, this time to the facilities of a local congregation in Seattle, Washington. Even though the curriculum was expanded and the setting had many practical advantages for students, enrollment remained low. Reluctantly the decision was made in January 1928 to close the school temporarily.

For the next fourteen years the church in the region was left with an educational void and a persistent hope that someday a school would again become a reality in the Northwest. Despite low enrollments, there had been widespread support for the school in several states and recognition of it by the national church as one of the three schools then existing in the United States, the others being Anderson Bible Training School (Anderson University) begun in 1917 and Kansas City Bible Training School begun in 1919. In fact, A. F. Gray was a member of the governing board of the college in Anderson for more than twenty years beginning in 1925 (serving as chair for more than a decade) and was recognized with an honorary doctorate from Anderson College in 1932. He was influenced by Church of God thinkers and writers like D. O. Teasley, A. D. Khan, and G. P. Tasker and in turn he was a great influence on the early and later development of the school in the Northwest.

Finally in September 1985 the Northwest Ministerial Assembly of the Church of God met in the First Church of God in Spokane which was being pastored by Rev. Henry Schlatter. The assembly developed new enthusiasm for the hope of a school and adopted unanimously the motion of Rev. E. V. Swinehart that again a college be established for training ministers. Excitement was evident and activity began.

By January 1936 the assembly had managed to buy back the old missionary home by paying its delinquent taxes. Now the college had a location and, following an election in September 1936, it had an official board of trustees. Rev. Schlatter of Spokane and Rev. A. F. Gray of Seattle sought funds to get the college off the ground while the whole country was trying to come out of a terrible depression. The legal incorporation of the new Pacific Bible College occurred in February 1937, with the corporation membership consisting of ministers of the Church of God in Washington,

Oregon, and Idaho. Classes began that October with fourteen students. The two faculty members were Daisy Maiden, a retired missionary from China, and A. F. Gray, who taught Bible, theology, psychology, Greek, and music in Spokane Tuesday through Friday while commuting on weekends by train to his pastorate in Seattle. Wilbur Skaggs, a young person in the Spokane congregation who was one of the first students, watched as the old "Saint's Home" was remodeled for use as a small college.

By 1938 Gray, again called to lead the school, had left his pastorate to devote full time to the college in Spokane. His wife, Rosa, served faithfully as college matron and cook while his son Harold ran the printing press in the basement and daughter Dorothy took classes and did secretarial work for the school. Mrs. Gray was cooking in the fall of 1938 for ten students from Washington, five from Oregon, four from California, three from Idaho, and one each from Kansas, Nebraska, and Oklahoma. The academic programs offered at this home on North Ash Street were a two-year course in Christian education, a three-year ministerial course, and a four-year degree course.

Then in 1940, with the student body having outgrown the available facilities in Spokane, the vacant Mountain View Sanitorium with about two acres of land in Portland, Oregon, was secured for what would become the long-term home of the college. That hillside structure would serve as library, dormitory, cafeteria, and administration building. The full purchase price of $14,000, a major financial obligation, was paid off in three years even though the total assets of the college amounted to only $5,400 when it moved from Spokane! This was a compelling symbol of Gray's inspired leadership and the presence in the area churches of people who obviously were committed to the mission of the school.

For the first years in Portland there were four teachers, Rev. Gray, Lottie Franklin, Pearl Lewis, and John Schmuki. The college was providing training primarily in Christian ministry, missions, religious education, and music. Slowly some adjacent properties were acquired. A dormitory for women was built in 1947 and a barracks was secured as war surplus to be used as a chapel. It was a modest, but a determined and a good beginning. Situated on the attractive southern slope of Mt. Tabor in Portland, the

Church of God in the Northwest had begun a significant investment in its educational vision.

The coming in 1942 of Dr. Otto F. Linn as faculty member and dean was one of the more significant events of the college's whole history. Linn, a nationally recognized biblical scholar and the first leader in the Church of God to earn a doctor's degree, came from a pastorate to give academic leadership to the young school. Earlier he had taught at Anderson College, but had left in part because of a disagreement with Dean Olt about the proper nature of curriculum in a church-related college. Although in the years to follow biblical study remained central in the curriculum and the school's primary purpose remained that of "training young men and women for definite religious service," by 1944 the Oregon State Department of Education had approved the granting of the Bachelor of Theology degree, with approval for the Bachelor of Arts soon to follow. The professional stature and leadership of Dean Linn were crucial for these developments.

The General Ministerial Assembly of the Church of God, meeting in Anderson, Indiana, in June 1947, approved the participation of the college in the national World Service annual distribution of contributed funds. Initially the college was to receive about six percent of the total or about thirty thousand dollars annually in those first years. Although question was raised about the appropriateness of the college sharing in the proceeds from general church giving when it did not function under the direct jurisdiction of the General Ministerial Assembly, it was agreed that it did function under the control of the West Coast Ministerial Assembly, did serve the entire church, and was prepared to function in close cooperation with the national church. By 1955 at least nineteen persons associated with the college already had or were serving on the mission fields of the world, a significant percentage of all Church of God missionaries.[2]

With an influx of veterans on campus, the student body grew to about two hundred. By 1951 the College catalog was able to list nineteen faculty members, including earned doctorates held by Otto F. Linn in Bible, D. S. Warner Monroe in philosophy, and C. Andreson Hubbard in biology. Others like Milo L. Chapman, Louis F. Gough, Irene Smith Caldwell, and John W. V. Smith were soon to complete doctorates and play major roles in this and other colleges of the Church of God. A major academic accomplishment was the building in 1954 of the Otto F. Linn Library. President Gray, naturally proud of these accomplishments and supportive of a broad curriculum of genuine academic quality, nonetheless wanted it to be clear that "this college is . . . a theological school. Its majors and minors are chosen in Bible, theology, Christian education, or music."[3] In the second verse of the college's alma mater are words expressing clearly the vision of the college which President Gray had molded over the years: "From thy stately portals issue, Ranks of stalwart youth; Forth to tell the gospel message, Heralds of the truth."

The end of an era and the beginnings of another in the college's history arrived during the 1950s. Because of failing health the beloved Dean Linn offered his resignation in 1955. He was succeeded by Milo Chapman, a faculty member in Old Testament and theology. In 1956, while completing a new men's residence hall, the college formally became a national agency of the Church of God. Although it had been receiving World Service funds since 1947, agency status meant that elections to the presidency of the college would require ratification by the General Ministerial Assembly. Also, college trustees, formerly elected by the West Coast Ministerial Assembly, would be elected by that national assembly. President Gray then announced his retirement in 1957 after fifty-two years of ministry in the Church of God. Dean Chapman was named to assume the presidency and faculty member Leslie Ratzlaff became dean.

To close out this most eventful decade, in 1959 the institution's name was changed from Pacific Bible College to Warner Pacific College. According to former faculty member and church historian John W. V. Smith, "this was more than a shift of labels. The new name allowed an enlargement of the curriculum to a full-orbed liberal arts program which would improve both student recruitment possibilities and the basis for approval by the regional accrediting association."[4] The college said that the new name was to honor Daniel S. Warner, "pioneer minister of the church . . . teacher, poet, author, printer . . . who understood holiness in ethical terms" and who was "a fervent advocate of the restoration of the true catholic church founded by Christ."⁵ A similar breadth of functions and lofty vision was intended for the college as well.

President Chapman, a trained scholar, experienced church leader, and educational philosopher, was able to lead a process that would capitalize on these increasing challenges and opportunities. New academic majors were added in history, English, and general education. Then in 1961, after careful preparation, accreditation was granted by the Northwest Association of Secondary and Higher Schools. This achievement was one of the larger of many gifts of leadership and hard work which Chapman managed to give to the college over the years. Chapman, a humble man with a love of teaching, decided, however, to return to the classroom full time at the end of his five-year term as president. An outpouring of love and appreciation came to him at the conclusion of his presidential term. His annual report of May 1962, the last of his presidency, carried a very positive tone. The accreditation had pleased him very much. The new gymnasium had been in use for several months, student enrollment was edging upward, and even the treasurer's report was guardedly optimistic.

The early sixties was a time of rapid growth in American higher education. Warner Pacific experienced something of that momentum. Dr. Louis F. Gough became the college's third president in 1962 after serving on the faculty of Anderson School of Theology in biblical studies and then as assistant to President Chapman from 1960-1962. He launched an expansion program on the occasion of the college's silver anniversary to raise an extra $250,000 to improve faculty salaries, expand library holdings, increase student financial aid, and maintain properly the campus facilities. By 1965, with the help of $100,000 authorized as a special project for the college by the General Ministerial Assembly, success was declared. Enrollment had increased from 177 students in 1960 to 338 in 1965. Library holdings went from about nineteen thousand to thirty thousand volumes. There were thirty full-time faculty members with twenty-eight percent holding the doctoral degree. A new dormitory for eighty-four students had been opened in 1964.

In 1964 Dr. Marvin Lindemuth, a prominent Washington educator and layperson, was installed as the fourth academic dean. The college joined the National Association of Intercollegiate Athletics and, with Cascade and George Fox Colleges, formed the

Associated Christian Colleges of Oregon. President Gough had announced at his inaugural the intent that "our college deepen and enrich its curriculum, strengthen and improve its processes of higher education in order that our campus may be characterized by academic excellence in every division of the liberal arts program." Dean Lindemuth stated in 1964:

> The Christian college is not a church but it is at its best when related to one. The church and its college have separate as well as shared responsibilities. The college is primarily an academic institution with its own unique task and function of providing opportunity for a liberal arts education within the Christian context.[6]

Respect was being sought through breadth and excellence of curriculum. Service was intended in the context of the larger life of the church. It was a stretching time.

Despite the troubled condition of American society in the mid-sixties (Vietnam war and civil rights movement), Warner Pacific anticipated a bright future. A long-range planning study led to the anticipation of seven hundred students by 1970 and an increasing role in the mainstream of Christian higher education. The board of trustees, feeling that the Portland campus had limited expansion potential and that the area was already oversupplied with colleges, was open to a new possibility when it received the offer of a gift of one hundred acres of land in San Jose, California. President Gough and the long-range planning committee favored accepting the gift and moving the campus to this site more central to the West Coast constituency. The trustees in April 1965 approved the recommendation to move and it also was approved that June by the General Ministerial Assembly in Anderson.

In the meantime discussion was carried on between Warner Pacific and Arlington College, the Southern California Association-sponsored school of the Church of God in Long Beach, about a possible merger of the colleges on the San Jose site. It appeared that a merger and a new campus were coming. But the dream as envisioned by the move's proponents collapsed. There were many persons, some Warner Pacific alumni, some ministers, and many Portland area residents, who opposed the move. There were strong feelings and genuine concern about the level of communication, the cost involved in the move, and even the solvency of the college in Portland. This produced widespread unrest and finally precipitated a crisis situation.

On June 7, 1966, President Gough, knowing that the consensus needed for the college to make the move no longer existed and feeling that his own influence and effectiveness had eroded seriously, submitted his resignation. Some felt that he had gone beyond what the college could afford. Others felt he could have managed the move if he had been more patient. The San Jose move was "temporarily" delayed and the college concentrated on raising money to cover its many unpaid bills in Portland. With a major effort and the sacrificial giving of many congregations and the national church and its agencies, the college survived the financial and relational crisis and remained in Portland. Arlington College, disappointed, would discover another merger possibility in the greater Los Angeles area (Azusa College). Former Warner Pacific president Milo Chapman had left Warner Pacific to teach at Arlington in 1964. He viewed with regret the failure of Warner Pacific and Arlington to unify the educational efforts of the Church of God on the West Coast.[7]

It was a difficult transition time. The financial challenge was significant. That summer Dr. Irene Caldwell, faculty member in Christian education for fourteen years, resigned to go to Anderson School of Theology, as did Dr. Kenneth Crose en route to the history faculty of Anderson College. Dean Lindemuth himself would leave to join Anderson College's education faculty in 1968. To varying degrees these and other changes resulted from professional and personal reasons as well as a range of reactions to the perceived instability and apparent direction being taken by Warner Pacific. Rev. E. Joe Gilliam, Indianapolis pastor and college trustee, was elected as the fourth president of the institution in 1966 and soon he invited Milo Chapman to return from Arlington to rejoin the faculty. There was need to bring new life to a campus which had come through some troubled waters and certainly had more yet lying ahead.

In the fall of 1966 the Warner board and the national church responded to a $300,000 emergency appeal for the unpaid and due bills of the college. President Robert H. Reardon of Anderson

A. Warner Memorial faculty and students, 1932-1933. **B.** Kansas City Bible Training School, 1918. **C.** Russell Byrum and James Massey. **D.** Commission on Christian Higher Education, 1978. **E.** C.C.H.E., 1987. **F.** C.C.H.E., 1959.

A. President Robert A. Nicholson, Anderson University. **B.** Former president John A. Morrison and students, Anderson College, 1953. **C.** President Nicholson announces new university status for Anderson, 1987. **D.** Gene Newberry, Earl Martin and School of Theology Students, 1952. **E.** A.C. welcomes Charles E. Wilson, Secretary of Defense for the United States, 1957. **F.** President Morrison and Dean Olt greet new S.O.T. dean, Adam W. Miller. **G.** Faculty and staff, Anderson College, 1952.

A. Instructor T. Cumberbatch and students, West Indies Theological College. **B.** Main building, West Indies Theological College. **C.** Arlington College Class for Ministers, 1964. **D.** W.I.T.C. Student in library. **E.** Herschell D. Rice, instructor, Arlington College, 1958. **F.** President DeWayne Bell (seated), Frederick Shackleton, Milo Chapman and Wilford Denton, Arlington, 1963.

A. President Robert C. Williams, Bay Ridge Christian College. **B.** First graduating class, B.R.C.C., 1974. **C.** Groundbreaking for first building, Bay Ridge, 1960. **D.** Construction on first building, B.R.C.C., 1961. **E.** Milking cows in college dairy, B.R.C.C. **F.** Students and faculty, B.R.C.C., 1965. **G.** Founder and first president, J. H. Germany, B.R.C.C.

A. President Robert J. Hazen, Gardner Bible College. **B.** Commencement procession, G.B.C., 1986. **C.** "Servant Song" singing group, G.B.C., 1986. **D.** Dean John A. Howard presenting Governor General of Canada award to Brenda Dormer, 1987. **E.** Service of celebration with the 1986 graduating class, G.B.C.

A. President John W. Conley, Mid-America Bible College. B. Oklahoma City campus, M.A.B.C. C. Opening day, South Texas Bible Institute, 1953. D. Dedication of library, Gulf-Coast Bible College, 1972; founding president, Max Gaulke, at right. E. Oklahoma governor George Nigh cuts ribbon at opening of M.A.B.C., 1985. F. First graduating class, G.B.C., 1958.

A. President Marshall K. Christensen, Warner Pacific College. **B.** Faculty, W.P.C., 1946. President A. F. Gray, left, rear. **C.** President Milo Chapman and Dean Leslie Ratzlaff, W.P.C., 1959. **D.** Dr. Lauren B. Sykes, teaching future music leaders, W.P.C., 1952. **E.** Librarian Ruth Green and student, Richard Hubacek, W.P.C., 1958. **F.** Dr. and Mrs. Warner Monroe, W.P.C.; Dr. Monroe was a long-time professor of philosophy.

A. President Leroy M. Fulton, Warner Southern College. **B.** Administrative leaders, W.S.C., 1972. **C.** Warner Southern Collegiate Chorale, 1985.
D. President Fulton and first graduate, Dan McCraw, W.S.C., 1972.
E. Groundbreaking, addition to Learning Resource Center, W.S.C., 1977.
F. W.S.C., confers honorary degrees on C. Carl Rainer and Edgar Williams, 1980.

College, chair of the Emergency Fund Committee, reported to pastors in November that the financial position of the Portland school had improved greatly from what it had been. The accrediting association extended for only one year the school's accreditation with a full self-study required the following year. The drive was on to re-establish confidence in college programs and personnel and to achieve financial stability for a debt-ridden institution plagued with several internal and external problems.

A financial consultant was secured and with his help efforts began to meet the expectations of a donor said to be capable and interested in making a multi-million dollar gift to the college. Stern measures were taken to find financial stability. Certain of these, such as ending the tenure program for faculty and introducing a more restricted approach to the liberal arts in favor of more vocationally and theologically oriented programs, were seen by some, including the dean, as detrimental to the integrity of the academic program. Dean Lindemuth was not the academic leader which President Gilliam saw as compatible with the new stress on more effective church relations and meeting the expectations of the prospective major donor. So Lindemuth left for Anderson College and Milo Chapman, beloved by Warner Pacific and the church, became dean.

It was indeed a hard time. Forty percent of the faculty did not return for the 1968-69 school year. But meaningful rebuilding was underway. The fall student enrollment of 1970 was up to a record 442. In June of that year the college requested and the General Assembly of the Church of God agreed to provide more special assistance, this time in the form of a guarantee of continuing World Service funding to discharge up to $600,000 of unsecured debt if the college should be unable to do so from its own resources. With creditors being reassured and President Gilliam providing aggressive leadership, there was optimism on campus for the future. The accrediting association, recognizing appropriate progress, reaffirmed the college's accreditation without time limitation. Dr. Earl McGrath, a national leader in higher education, in his address at Warner's 1971 commencement praised President Gilliam for giving "leadership in this hour of crisis for all colleges."

Gilliam sought a broadening of the base of guidance and support for the college. Believing that the college was to penetrate all of society and not function as an ingrown sect, he established a College Advisory Board which was to include Ralph G. Turnbull, Evelyn Egtvedt, Paul S. Rees, D. Elton Trueblood, Earl J. McGrath and Lowell J. Williamson. With the generous assistance of the Kellogg Foundation and the Lilly Endowment and the guidance of McGrath, the faculty designed an innovative liberal arts program known as the "Culture of Western Man." The number of academic majors was reduced from sixteen to eleven, and in 1973 the college launched a Master of Religion degree program (expansion of the earlier five-year Bachelor of Theology degree) with pastor/writer Ralph Turnbull as a supporting scholar in residence. Turnbull also was influential in the campus launching in 1974 an annual Christian Writers' Conference that was to gain national prominence in the years to follow.

These program developments, unfortunately, were plagued by the continuing problem of functioning beyond available resources. The multi-million dollar gift from a private donor finally did materialize, but in the form of a long-term trust not immediately available for operational support. Business leaders were added to the advisory board as well as political leaders such as Congresswoman Edith Green and Oregon's Senator Mark Hatfield. Even United States President Gerald Ford visited the campus as a commencement speaker in May 1976. Properties adjacent to the campus were acquired for future development through a major grant from the Murdock Trust.

The casual observer would have judged campus progress to have been substantial and enviable during the 1970s. The number of graduates grew. There was significant improvement in campus facilities. But there was an undercurrent that was quietly ominous. Operational deficits were persistent and threatened the viability of the institution. A series of personnel and program decisions over the years had created a pool of ill will in various quarters. The visibility of the advisory board caused some ministers and even members of the Board of Trustees to feel that an informal group of hand-picked, "outside" persons were inappropriately in charge of the school's direction and destiny. Then in 1979 all of this concern and criticism surfaced in a local newspaper article that ignited widespread discussion and turmoil.[8]

It had been little more than a decade since a Warner Pacific president found it necessary to resign in the midst of crippling controversy. Now in 1979 it happened again. This newspaper article was characterized by President Gilliam as the result of an unresolved grievance between the college and a former employee and as one which had not portrayed him as the sort of man he was or would ever want to be. Whatever the real facts and the level of the article's unfairness, Gilliam soon resigned and was replaced by Dr. Milo Chapman. The national church's Division of World Service was convinced to suspend temporarily its normal fund-raising limitations so that an urgent $300,000 appeal could be made directly by the college to congregations in the western states.

Why the large and perennial operational deficits? Board chair Jay Barber suggested that it was a pattern of smaller student enrollments than budgets were based upon, too heavy a reliance on the excellent fund-raising abilities of President Gilliam to cover whatever financial shortfalls there might be, and even an unconscious reliance on the eventual availability of that multi-million dollar trust from the private donor.[9] The Church of God constituency in the Northwest was not large and, as President Gough had observed years earlier, the Portland area was well populated with competitive institutions of higher education. Even so, many persons believed deeply in the mission of the college and were prepared to help find a way into the future.

That future was to be guided by Dr. Marshall Christensen who had come to Warner Pacific as a student in 1960, then became a faculty member in 1966, an academic leader under President Gilliam, and finally president in 1981. As a former Fulbright scholar in Germany and the first layperson chosen to serve as president of any Church of God college, Christensen had great faith in the mission of a Christian college. As a highly trained scholar, he was prepared to pursue that faith with academic integrity and considerable energy. There surely was much to be done.

A three-year plan was set forth. The college had passed through a difficult transition in leadership and now looked at the decade of the 1980s as one in which the college would reach its fiftieth year (1987). During this decade the college would make every effort to increase student enrollment, become a leader in curriculum innovation among Christian liberal arts institutions, and be recognized as a significant educational resource in Portland and the Pacific Northwest. Obviously this would require much creativity and an expanding base of persons who would be challenged by this cause and motivated to give the needed support. A central part of the plan was to put the operating and capital budgets of the college on a path of stability and real growth. It indeed had to be a time for a new beginning.

By 1984 the annual report of President Christensen celebrated several ways in which God had been blessing the college. In that year Dr. Joyce Erickson, a nationally recognized educator, had come to campus as Dean of Faculty. There also had been a thirty-seven percent increase in the number of freshmen and transfer students. A new five-year plan of action had been launched and a multi-million dollar "Investing in People" capital funds campaign designed to bring significant reduction in the burden of continuing institutional debt and a sizable increase in the small institutional endowment. It was reported that efforts at disciplined management of resources allowed the audit for the year ending June 1983 to be the fourth in a row to show a modest surplus in the operational budget.

Excellent media coverage of the college in the Portland area had been a plus in public relations. Innovative programming such as the hearing and speech theraphy program for preschool children and the Bethlehem Inn for homeless families highlighted the campus concern for human needs locally. President Christensen was becoming known and appreciated across the Church of God as a strong educational leader and a wise and committed churchman.

The future is still a major challenge. While there now are rays of light on the horizon, financial deficits remain a real problem. Debt from the past is proving a heavy burden on the present. New constituencies and sources of income must be found.

The campus and the whole Church of God celebrated the college's fiftieth anniversary during 1986-1987 and, despite problems, looked ahead in faith.

Notes

[1] *Gospel Trumpet,* September 4, 1919, p. 23.
[2] Donald D. Johnson, B. D. Thesis, "An Historical Survey of the Church of God in the Pacific Northwest," Anderson School of Theology, 1955, p. 448.
[3] Ibid., p. 446.
[4] John W. V. Smith, *The Quest For Holiness and Unity* (Anderson, Indiana: Warner Press, 1980), pp. 367-368.
[5] In *Warner World,* Warner Pacific College, October 25, 1962, p. 3.
[6] From essay titled "A Christian College Faces the Future" published by Warner Pacific College, 1964.
[7] Milo Chapman in taped interview with Barry Callen, February 25, 1980.
[8] "A College Led Astray" by Kathie Durbin in *Willamette Week,* October 9, 1978.
[9] Interview highlighted in *Vital Christianity,* March 25, 1979, pp. 20-21.

Table 9
Warner Pacific College (Portland, Oregon)

Institutional Names:
 1937-1959 Pacific Bible College
 1959-   Warner Pacific College
           In 1940 the college was moved from Spokane, Washington, to Portland, Oregon.

Accreditations:
 1961-   Northwest Association of Colleges and Schools

Chief Executive Officers:
 1937-1957 Albert F. Gray
 1957-1962 Milo L. Chapman
 1962-1966 Louis F. Gough
 1966-1979 E. Joe Gilliam
 1979-1981 Milo L. Chapman
 1981-   Marshall K. Christensen

Chief Academic Officers:
 1937-1942 Albert F. Gray (while president)
 1942-1955 Otto F. Linn
 1955-1957 Milo L. Chapman
 1958-1963 Leslie W. Ratzlaff
 1963-1964 Marvin H. Lindemuth (acting)
 1964-1968 Marvin H. Lindemuth
 1968-1973 Milo L. Chapman
 1973-1975 Curtis Loewen
 1975-1978 Marshall K. Christensen
 1978-1981 Thomas N. Pappas
 1981-1983 Louis G. Foltz
 1983-1987 Joyce Erickson
 1987-   Edward Whitehead (acting)

Current Chair, Governing Board:
 1988-   John Thompson

Chapter 10
The Story of Warner Southern College

Talk about the possibility of a "southern college" began in 1945 at the Jacksonville, Florida, meeting of the Southern Convention of the Church of God. Such talk was to continue for the next twenty years before a series of concrete actions were taken that actually led to the establishment of a new institution of higher education within the life of the Church of God.

Why was there such persistent interest in this possibility by some church leaders despite the many frustrating years of exploration and the great difficulties involved in realizing such a dream? Distance was one reason often stated. Anderson College in Indiana seemed so far away from several of the southern states. Travel was slow and expensive forty years ago. Another reason was a regional concern. Young persons who did go north for college often remained in the North. So it seemed reasonable, even crucial, to many persons that there should be a southern college. It was expected that such a school in the area would develop new leadership, particularly ministerial leadership, and thereby bring increased strength to the Church of God in the South.

WARNER
SOUTHERN COLLEGE

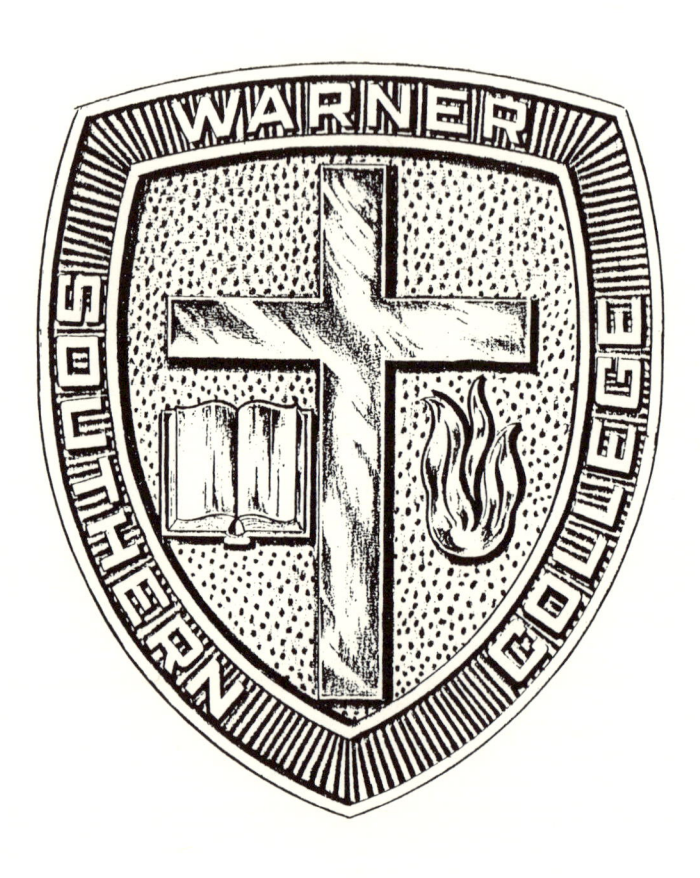

What originally was envisioned as a practical way to begin was not a new and independent institution, but an extension of Anderson College. In this way the new educational venture could, from its beginning, be an accredited and respected school connected to the larger life of the Church of God. Charlie Cheeks, a key person in these conversations from their beginning, said that "we never had a thought of starting an independent college."

Cheeks, from Mississippi, graduated from Anderson College in 1945. He had worked for both the Gospel Trumpet Company (now Warner Press) and Anderson College and carried a burden for ministerial education, particularly in the South and particularly to assist disadvantaged Black young persons in the church. Returning to pastor in Alabama in 1945, he and others encouraged the idea of an extension college and he was in an especially good position to work closely with officials at Anderson College in an attempt to realize such a possibility.

Dean Russell Olt of Anderson College expressed interest, but there were many practical questions to be answered. By 1948 Cheeks was again employed by Anderson College as a fund raiser and soon was involved in raising money for its first major dormitory, Morrison Hall. But his personal interest in the South remained strong, and soon he moved to South Carolina to pastor. Meanwhile, the Southern Convention discussions about a college possibility had continued on a sporadic basis. Pastors like Henry Johnson from Mississippi, Harry Harp from Georgia, and Fred Vines from Alabama acted together to explore and promote the idea of a college in the South. Johnson preached in 1949 for Malcolm Rigel, then pastoring in Indiana, and shared the vision with him. Six years later Rigel returned to the South to pastor.

In 1953 the Southern Convention appointed a nine-member committee to study the need for a Church of God college in the Southeast. Several members were Anderson College graduates who saw the importance of education and were anxious that something be done. Progress was slow, however, and by 1957, another committee was appointed. It was comprised of Charlie Cheeks, then pastoring in Florida, and designated committee chair, Joseph Benson, an elementary school principal in Florida, and Arlo Newell, a pastor in North Carolina. These men proceeded to explore again the problems and the possibilities. Momentum was building toward some kind of action. President John Morrison and Dean Russell Olt of Anderson College were supportive of the process of exploration. In February 1958 a group of the state assembly chairs of the Church of God gathered in Florida and went away promising to seek some underwriting of such a project from their states. A brochure was printed which announced the coming of the "Southeastern Extension Center of Anderson College."

Cheeks was now pastoring in Columbia, South Carolina. In March of 1958 he hosted a meeting of forty area ministers and Robert A. Nicholson, assistant to the dean of Anderson College. Plans were laid for a beginning, an initial summer session of the Extension Center. Operational details were worked out with Nicholson by June. The basic design was for the center to be sponsored by the Southern Convention with Anderson College providing the academic administration, faculty, library resources, and credits.

This first summer term began on June 30, 1958, with Cheeks as coordinator and Dr. Burt Coody teaching the two courses offered, one in Bible, and one in psychology. The six students were housed by Cheeks. Each of them finished the summer with six hours of credit granted by Anderson College.

Two additional summer terms were held in Birmingham, Alabama, in 1959 and 1960. They used the facilities of the Pinehurst Church of God congregation and the camp meeting grounds, with about fifteen students attending each term. Admission requirements and academic policies were those of Anderson College. Felix Murrell and Marie Strong taught in 1959 and Donald Courtney and Florence Orr in 1960. Local layman Carl Raines hosted the teachers in his home. Robert Nicholson, then dean of Anderson College, was present for the launching of each term.

This center, however, had its obvious limitations. It seemed only temporary to the students, causing them to question its usefulness for their long-term educational needs. Among some ministers, strong feelings surfaced about the appropriateness of a potentially racially integrated student body in the face of the heated racial tensions of the time. For these and probably other reasons, there was too little money pledged and too few students preregistered to justify the center's functioning in 1961.

But the end was not yet. The years 1961-1963 were ones of wrestling with the concept of the center and a search for its most appropriate location. The concept developed into the hope for a two-year junior college tied closely to Anderson College. Three possible sites were considered in the states of North Carolina, Arkansas, and Florida. Enthusiasm, frustration, and general turmoil were the end result.

An old campus in Red Springs, North Carolina, became available. James Burchett, then chair of the Southern Convention, convened church leaders on the site in August of 1962, and an option for its purchase went before the Southern Convention in November. It lost amidst considerable emotion about a range of issues. What was approved was a resolution naming a Southern Commission on Higher Education (including the convention officers) "to give direction to such programs of action and study as this Convention shall initiate and to give direction in the soliciting and expenditure of funds for these purposes." The new commission was charged to "give continuing study to the possibility of establishing some type of college in the South" because of the assumption that "the progress and growth of the Church of God in the South lies in training and educating today's youth and that to invest in them at this crucial point in our history is the best hope for the future."

The new commission met in Anderson, Indiana, in January 1963. It heard and decided against a substantial offer to host a new college made by the Industrial Development Committee of Eldorado, Arkansas. It reported to the church's national Commission on Christian Higher Education, also in session in Anderson, and tried to clarify past actions and future intent.

The Southern Commission on Higher Education next met that March in Jacksonville, Florida, since an offer of prime land in that city had been received. Because this appeared an exceptionally attractive offer, the commission set a strategy for sharing information and building support for this option in the coming months. Then in November the Southern Convention debated the issue for nearly a day.

Supporters of the Jacksonville opportunity were vocal and strongly committed. But others feared the financial obligation or thought that the site was not centrally located or didn't want to encourage the birth of a weak and unaccredited college or argued that the Southern Convention, a fellowship assembly, was not an appropriate sponsoring body. All agreed that a vote of at least eighty-five percent should be required to accept the Jacksonville offer. The affirmative vote was seventy-six percent, bringing strong disappointment to many. Some of the ministers gave up in the face of this recurrent inability to ever take definitive action together. Too many agendas were involved.

Malcolm Rigel, who had just accepted a pastorate in Jacksonville in anticipation of the proposed school there, took his own action. He sent a letter to the ministers insisting that "this issue is not dead. We are going to get a structure started!" He then organized a meeting in Florida a month later so that a group could look prayerfully to the future. About twenty persons came, including Leslie Ratzlaff, former dean of Warner Pacific College in Portland, Oregon, and the new pastor in Fort Lauderdale, Florida. At this meeting, Ratzlaff presented his concept of a "unique Christian college."

Now there was new hope that the Jacksonville option might be accepted after all. Soon the Florida Ministerial Assembly set in motion a process that convened in April 1964, in Jacksonville, about sixty persons who were burdened to see a college founded. The hope was that the Jacksonville property option might still be accepted by a grouping of Church of God leaders other than the Southern Convention. But before the meeting convened, and unknown to those involved, the convention chair formally rejected the Jacksonville offer and thereby ended the opportunity altogether! This was a severe blow, but the meeting was to be significant nonetheless.

What happened was the establishment of the Southeastern Association of the Church of God. It was to be chartered in Florida and exist as a legal body for the sole purpose of establishing a college. Kenneth Cleary, an attorney from Bradenton, Florida, was a new Christian and had become involved through his pastor. He prepared a proposed constitution and bylaws for the new college that called for a Board of Trustees of ten ministers and eleven laypersons from the Southeast. The bylaws were adopted and the first board members were elected.

Ratzlaff, asked to serve as a consultant because of his considerable educational training and experience, presented a written "Prospectus on a Southern College." His vision was of a distinctly Christian college, four-year in scope, designed specifically for area needs. It should be, he wrote, a college "in the South, that understands the South and that supplies Christian leadership for the church in the South." Possibly because he himself had served previously in Grand Cayman and Jamaica, and certainly because of the potential of a Florida location, he also emphasized the Caribbean and Latin America as within the scope of the particular mission of such a college.

By now the long-term assumption that an extension campus of Anderson College was the goal had changed. Many factors, probably including the experience and particular vision of Ratzlaff, the major involvement of laypersons like Cleary (new to the Church of God), the Florida setting in which the state already was committed to providing a junior or community college option to its citizens at very low cost, and the belief that Anderson College was not in favor of a southern college brought the change. The concern for regional relevance and regional control was strong.

The college board soon elected two laypersons, Kenneth Cleary and Richard Smith, as chair and vice-chair, organized into committees, and continued the search for a site. Several were considered in different parts of Florida. Finally, a gift of 350 acres of property in a rural area near Lake Wales in central Florida was chosen, although there was opposition. Pastoral members Malcolm Rigel, Leroy Fulton, and Ernest Gross opposed this choice in early votes of the board, but finally decided to go along with the majority despite concern about its rural location.

Board chair Cleary went to Anderson in January 1965 to report to the national Commission on Christian Higher Education. He shared the intended nature and scope of the coming college and the hope that it would function cooperatively with the whole church. What he heard in return was a series of probing questions about the wisdom and feasibility of such a venture. But the decision to proceed was firm and would not be altered despite the questions and concerns of many national church leaders.

A call for financial support went out to the churches in the

South. At a crucial board meeting in Cordelle, Georgia, on May 6, 1966, Leroy Fulton, then pastor in Sarasota, Florida, was elected new board chair. Malcolm Rigel remained secretary and Leslie Ratzlaff was asked to leave his pastorate and become the administrator who would actually organize and start the college near Lake Wales. Soon Charlie Cheeks was assisting in various ways as work began to bring the dream to reality. In November 1966 the Southern Convention went on record as favoring the recent decisions and encouraged the churches to become supportive.

Work began in earnest. Property became available for a new local congregation. Books for a library came from a closed library in Miami and from Arlington College in California (merging with Azusa Pacific College). Six thousand volumes had been processed and were ready for use the day the college opened, with Nina Ratzlaff having assumed responsibility for the library's operation. Hersel and Eula Studebaker moved to Lake Wales to start a mobile home manufacturing plant so that students could have employment—crucial in that rural setting. Charlie Cheeks, the O. M. Richardsons, and Harold White established College Park, a mobile home park adjacent to the college which was hoped would attract Church of God retirees from the North.

Finally the college got its name. In November 1967 the Board adopted the name Warner Southern College, "Warner" relating to the Church of God and "Southern" to the region of the country to be served. This name was the suggestion of Dr. Ratzlaff who earlier had suggested "Warner Pacific College" as the new name for Pacific Bible College in Portland, Oregon. The next month the first building was under construction through the generosity of trustee Carl Raines.

Ratzlaff, an experienced academic leader, planned the new academic program and reported progress to the national commission on Christian Higher Education in January 1967. There he heard continuing reservations about the wisdom of starting another college in the church. In fact, this commission reported to the General Assembly of the Church of God the next June that the Church of God already had enough colleges and could not support more.

But in the South there was no turning back. Classes were scheduled to begin in the fall of 1968. Pastor Ero Moore of Lake Placid,

Florida, took a leave of absence to recruit students and raise money for the college. Malcolm Rigel moved to Lake Wales to pastor the new Kingdom Builder church and be dean of students. Leslie Ratzlaff worked at communicating clearly his own intention. He wrote:

> An accredited . . . college is on the way. Accredited by God, in that it is to be thoroughly Christian; accredited by higher education in that is it to be academically sound!

Classes began on schedule with twenty-seven students enrolled. Of the seventeen full-time students, thirteen were from Florida. Another one thousand volumes arrived for the library from faculty members at Anderson College who were moving their offices into mobile units so that Decker Hall could be constructed on the site of "Old Main." An excellent faculty was assembled, all part-time, but four with doctoral degrees. Some, like Charles Bates, drove a long distance to teach a night class. Reverend Malcolm Rigel, the local pastor, was dean of students. Reverend Ernest Gross, pastoring in Orlando, Florida, assisted in the classroom. Faculty members Charles Bates, Florence Orr Barnett, and Cecil Hartselle had all taught previously at Anderson College, the latter two having retired. It was a small but quality beginning.

That first year was characterized by a close family atmosphere. In spite of the limited beginnings a representative from the regional accrediting body, the Southern Association of College and Schools, was invited to examine the situation and give direction the summer after the first year of operation. This was evidence of Dr. Ratzlaff's tenacious commitment to quality in academics. He always couped this commitment with a careful screening of faculty candidates in regard to compatibility with the Christian mission of the college.

During that first year of operation, the board met to offer a formal position to Charlie Cheeks. There were questions about what the title would be and how the positions would relate to that of Dr. Ratzlaff. It was decided that a president should be named. Consideration was given to Cheeks and Malcolm Rigel, but Rigel nominated board chair Leroy Fulton, Sarasota pastor and graduate of Anderson College and its School of Theology. The board elected Fulton, who expressed the desire not to assume office until 1970 after a year of graduate study in college administration. So the board agreed to name Cheeks president for a year with Fulton being president-elect until July 1970. While Cheeks was considering this proposed arrangement, he suffered a heart attack. So the board convinced Fulton to assume the presidency in July 1969. Under his executive leadership and the academic leadership of Dr. Ratzlaff, the college grew rapidly from very modest beginnings.

By the 1974-1975 school year, the student enrollment had increased to 187. They came from twenty states, with Florida leading the way and Ohio next, and six foreign countries (eleven students mostly from the Caribbean islands). Significant persons joined the faculty, including Edgar Williams and Perry Grubbs in 1970, and Dr. Robert Clark in 1971. Dr. Charles Bates became full time in 1972, and Rev. Harold Boyer, prominent leader in the Church of God, joined the teaching staff that same year. These and others, including Dr. Irene Caldwell who came in 1973 after retiring from Anderson School of Theology, Dr. Ronald Jack, who came in 1974 and was to become dean when Ratzlaff retired in 1983, Sam Wellman (1974) and Wade Jakeway (1975) were beginning to make major contributions.

This growth in enrollment and faculty was paralleled by program development and an expanding library of exceptional quality for a small, young college. Accreditation was a major goal and the foundation was being laid carefully. In 1972 correspondent status was granted by the Southern Association of Colleges and Schools, with candidate status to follow the next year. Buildings were built and properties improved. A quality business office operation had to be designed and implemented. All of this went forward on the east side of U.S. 27 (which divides the campus property) although the long-range plan was to build the main campus on the larger section of land on the west side.

Income and total college assets rose steadily. Finances always were a struggle, but the college managed to pay its bills and students found the necessary employment. By 1977 there were twenty-three buildings on campus, including a library of about fifty thousand volumes and several homes and mobile units. Then, in December 1977, full accreditation was granted. The campus rejoiced and morale was high. It was a major accomplishment for a college in only its tenth year of operation.

It was hoped that accreditation would result in a significant increase in student enrollment, but this did not happen. The college sought to be innovative by working on other fronts to build a larger financial and student base. By the end of 1985-1986, eleven academic majors were offered, concentrating in church ministries, teacher education, business administration, social services, and international development and missions. Included in the 1987 graduating class were fifty persons receiving the Bachelor of Arts degree and eleven the Associate of Arts degree. Of these, twenty-two were in teacher education and nineteen in fields related to church ministries.

The "HEART" program, training persons to live and serve in underdeveloped countries, was gaining a national reputation. Attempts were made to organize and build a condominium community near campus. Progress finally was made on the development of the new campus on the west side of the highway, with a dormitory completed and an academic-recreational complex under construction. But the president's report for 1985-1986, with all of the positives, carried a basic note of continuing caution: ". . . the concerns are always the same—students, finance, faculty, and staff."

Originally the intent behind the existence of Warner Southern had been the founding of an extension of Anderson College in the South. The eventual result was an independent, four-year Christian college in the liberal arts tradition, with an educational philosophy very similar to that of what is now called Anderson University. Ties with Anderson College, however, remained close over these years. This was particularly true of the graduate School of Theology to which many Warner Southern graduates went for seminary training (their success in this graduate school was helpful in Warner Southern gaining its accreditation in 1977). This relationship was highlighted even further in 1983 with the establishment of the seminary's extension on the Warner Southern campus. Dean Barry Callen of the School of Theology developed this extension program with Dean Leslie Ratzlaff of Warner Southern. It was a continuing of the tradition of an extension relationship that went back to 1958. In 1986 the School of Theology granted six Master of Arts in Religion degrees to persons from the Florida extension. By 1988, however, the constituency for this extension had dropped to a level that led to the decision to cease its operation.

Warner Southern College has worked hard at being relevant to the needs of the Church of God, particularly in the Southeast and in the Caribbean, a task central to its founding purpose. The limitation of resources has been an ongoing challenge, and the need for students did lead to serious recruitment efforts in the Midwest where the Church of God population is much larger. Ohio, for instance, has been a major source of students for the college over the years.

The problems faced by Warner Southern since its beginning have tended to be seen as expected hurdles which every young college must clear somehow. Persons have been willing to serve and sacrifice over many years. Included are Ero Moore, a key staff person since 1968; J. Perry Grubbs who was with the college from 1970-1986 as a music faculty member and then vice-president for development; Donald Pickett; Wesley Rouse; and others. Also to be noted, of course, are the long and distinguished tenures of Leroy Fulton as president, Leslie Ratzlaff as dean, and Nina Ratzlaff in library services. But the opening of the 1987-1988 school year saw several significant faculty persons absent because of retirement. Included in this one year were Dr. Harold Boyer, Dr. Robert Clark, Dr. Deryl Johnson, Dr. Fred Morgan, and Dr. Malcolm Rigel. Clearly it was a challenging time of transition.

The college has remained closely tied over the years to the Southern Convention of the Church of God and has been represented regularly in the national Commission on Christian Higher Education. However, it never has become a national agency college like Anderson, Mid-America, and Warner Pacific. This status has not been sought actively for several reasons. In the early years it was mostly a matter of keeping faith with a promise that the church at large would not be asked to take responsibility for the new college. While the college's board has taken no position on the matter, in more recent years interest has been expressed by President Fulton that this possibility be given some objective consideration. Some persons outside the college have suggested that the limitations imposed by agency status might be to the college's disadvantage or that one more college agency might overbalance higher education's share of the World Service budget and thus trigger an entirely new way for all of the colleges to relate to this budget of the general church. But whatever the reality of advantages or disadvantages, no formal consideration of agency status has developed to date.

A major issue for Warner Southern College now is its concern that the total Church of God in the United States develop an increasing sense of its ownership of the college. Although this ownership has not yet evidenced itself in any structural or financial arrangement at the national level, the college has worked openly and constructively with many aspects of the life of the Church of God nationally and regionally. And it certainly has contributed to it. The dilemma to be faced may be how a college with a founding mission of serving a particular region of the country can be successful in gaining such ownership, particularly when its founding was seen as unwise by many at the national level.

President Fulton tended to speak for the many faculty and staff members of the college over the years when he recalled:

> My happy times have been seeing students graduate and go on to be involved in ministry. A short time ago I ran across my roll book for the freshman Church of God doctrine class for 1972-1973. Of the 55 in the class, fifteen now work in missions or church ministry, nine are wives of pastors, six are teaching, some are in social work. It is a real joy to see persons involved in ministry around the world.

By 1987 the college had graduated a total of 633 persons who were serving in Argentina, Bermuda, Brazil, Canada, El Salvador, Grand Cayman, Grenada, Haiti, Honduras, Japan, Kenya and, of course, the United States. That same year was the one in which "Year 20" was celebrated and the highest enrollment in the college's history was enjoyed. The future would not be easy, but neither was the past when so much had been accomplished against great odds.

Table 10
Warner Southern College
(Lake Wales, Florida)

Institutional Names:
  1968-   Warner Southern College
Accreditations:
  1977-   Southern Association of Colleges and Schools
Chief Executive Officers:
  1968-1969 Leslie W. Ratzlaff
  1969-   Leroy M. Fulton
Current Chair of Governing Board:
  1977-   Kenneth W. Cleary

Chapter 11
The Story of
West Indies Theological College

The Caribbean region includes many islands, many nations. Those which are English-speaking were former British colonies that have gained their independence. Unfortunately, a rather narrow insular mentality has characterized many relationships among these island nations. The missionary work of the Church of God in this region, consequently, has tended to develop similarly, with each nation having its own leaders, leadership structure, and program priorities. Efforts at leadership training, often related to institutions and academic leaders of the church in the United States, have not managed to survive the disadvantages of such a lack of integrated effort toward a common goal. The Missionary Board in the United States has sought to be a unifying force, and the recently evolved Caribbean Atlantic Assembly is an expression of the church in the region seeking a means to make unified ministry a growing reality.

Two institutions of higher education emerged, the first in Jamaica, the second in Trinidad and Tobago. One no longer exists; the other is struggling to survive and find its way to a more productive future.

WEST INDIES THEOLOGICAL COLLEGE

THY WORD GIVETH LIGHT

PORT OF SPAIN, TRINIDAD, W.I.

Jamaica School of Theology

During the early years of the work of the Church of God in Jamaica, the church had no system of theological training for ministers and other leaders except what missionary Nellie Olson managed to provide in the Kingston Sunday school. But soon she became burdened for a Bible school and was encouraged in this when, in 1921, J. W. Phelps, secretary-treasurer of the Missionary Board in the United States, visited Jamaica. A furlough followed which allowed Mrs. Olson to complete a two-year ministerial course in the new Anderson Bible Training School and Seminary in Anderson, Indiana (now Anderson University). When she returned to Jamaica in 1924, she was both better prepared and more determined than ever to start a school.

The Jamaica Bible Institute was opened in January 1926 in Kingston. Classes for the original five students were held in the High Holborn Street chapel with Nellie Olson as principal and the only teacher. A four-year theological course was outlined and the purpose was stated as the preparation of young men and women for Christian service. The institute was operated under the auspices of the Missionary Board in the United States, but there was a local guidance committee that included Jamaicans. It was hoped that the institute would serve the needs of persons from Jamaica, Barbados, Trinidad, and elsewhere in the Caribbean. Ambitious plans were laid in faith despite the scarcity of resources. Soon small cash gifts began arriving from concerned persons in Cuba, Panama, and the United States.

In the second year of operation, Alva Ramsey was engaged to assist in the teaching. Arithmetic, Latin, and Spanish were taught for assistance with the Junior Cambridge examination, with geometry and algebra to follow for those preparing for the Senior Cambridge exam. This enabled the development of a level of academic achievement recognized and valued by the Jamaican and neighboring societies of the time. Also during this year Edith Young was sent to Jamaica by the Missionary Board. She spent her entire career teaching in the institute, retiring in 1964.

By 1929 the institute was gaining in strength and general recognition. Eleven acres of land were purchased facing Ardenne Road and Hope Road in a suburban section of Kingston for the use of the institute. In 1930 the first three students completed the four-year course and were graduated. Nine more were to be so honored by 1942. Although the numbers were small, the accomplishment was meaningful to the life of the church. Primarily it was the vision, faith, and perseverance of Nellie Olson, the institute's founder and first principal, that made it all possible.

During this initial phase of the institute's history, a major problem developed. There was in the region a great demand for schools that would enable persons to gain a secondary education that permitted passage of the Cambridge exams and thus opened doors for employment in many fields. Since the institute provided this educational service, that function grew more quickly than that related more specifically to leadership training for the church. So, partly to enhance the primary reason for the institute's existence, in 1938 the two departments were separated into two institutions, Jamaica Bible Institute facing Hope Road, and Ardenne High School facing Ardenne Road. By 1940 Mary Olson, daughter of George and Nellie, was principal of Ardenne High School and Charles and Florence Struthers were sent by the Missionary Board in 1946 to devote their time to the institute.

Now the institute was offering three courses of study: a short-term Christian Education program; a two-year gospel workers program; and, for an additional two years, the ministerial training program. Students who needed financial assistance for room and board worked in maintaining the property or in the agricultural and industrial projects of the institute. Over these years, many students came and then went back into the life of the church. Both missionaries (like Raymond and Elna Mae Hastings, Leslie and Nina Ratzlaff, and Edith Young) and local Jamaican leaders taught and otherwise contributed to the work of the institute.

The Jamaican society was developing rapidly and eager for educational progress. Standards and expectations were rising. So the question kept coming: How can Jamaica Bible Institute graduate more highly qualified students? W. W. King wrote from Anderson in 1959 that "plans are now being worked out to upgrade the school as the growing need for leaders demands." Part of that plan turned out to be Kenneth Jones, a young American minister-educator who spent 1960 as mission secretary in Jamaica. He traveled and preached in the churches and served on the governing boards of the institute and high school. He came to understand the challenge and to develop a strategy for further development of the work in Jamaica.

After two years pastoring back in the United States, Jones was asked by the Missionary Board to return to Jamaica to reorganize the institute and be its principal. He and his family arrived with a strengthened curricular design and a desire to help work out some of the organizational problems hindering the possible expansion of the institute's work. In a series of meetings, the basic concepts were conveyed and accepted by the institute's board. But then Mrs. Jones fell ill and the family was forced to return home, delaying the opening of a new school term.

James E. Massey of Detroit, Michigan, was appointed to become the new principal and see that the institute was opened again. He and his wife arrived in January 1964. According to Jones, Massey "went to fit into the new organization and carry out my plan." Under Massey's leadership, the institute did indeed experience a new day and a new enthusiasm. There was stress on achieving a serious educational environment. The aim was to lift the academic program to the level where students could be tutored to take the external examinations for the Diploma in Theology or the Bachelor of Divinity from London University. The curriculum was to be operated at a university level with passage of the Senior Cambridge exam expected for admission.

Surely this was a new day which justified a new and more appropriate name for the school. So the more prestigious name Jamaica School of Theology became effective in April 1964. There was excitement and momentum. The student body of thirteen was large by local standards and several of its faculty members were Jamaicans. Indeed, as a result of the intensified curriculum, there were students who passed the difficult external examinations. Persons with London degrees were considered genuinely educated and could enroll for higher degrees in almost any college or university in Great Britain or the United States. Some did just that, becoming the pride of Principal Massey and leaders wherever they went. In the background but supporting much of this academic thrust throughout this time was the school's vocational department. Led by Ralph Little, it provided the needed employment for many of the students.

It was the conviction of Massey that the cost of quality theological education was far more than the Jamaican church could afford alone or that the American church should be expected to bear. So he encouraged leaders "to be forward-looking and see the importance of an ecumenical venture in this regard." An opportunity and a major decision arose.

George and Nellie Olson, first missionaries to Jamaica, had been progressive and ecumenically-minded Christians. For instance, under George's influence many years earlier, the Church of God had become a charter member of the Jamaica Council of Churches. Nellie had always welcomed to the institute students from many denominational backgrounds. Now, in 1964, Jamaica School of Theology was reaching for quality programming with a small student body and inadequate resources. Several other theological schools in the country were facing the same dilemma.

An ecumenical plan developed that called for the formation of the United Theological College of the West Indies. It would combine resources in one institution, operate in Kingston in close relationship with the University of the West Indies, and offer a Licentiate in Theology comparable to the Diploma in Theology from London University. The Church of God was invited to assist financially in this joint venture with the understanding that a proportional number of Church of God students could attend. Classes and requirements would be the same for all cooperating schools except where distinctive denominational doctrines required a special class and qualified instructor.

This plan offered a way to further strengthen instruction and achieve accreditation for Jamaica School of Theology. But the majority of Church of God leaders in Jamaica were hesitant. They were concerned about the possible loss of their own identity and influence in such an ecumenical setting, particularly because of the Roman Catholic presence in the United Theological College. They questioned the wisdom of Church of God ministerial students training under largely non-Church of God instructors. So in December 1964 the offer to join in the venture was declined by the Church of God in Jamaica. Massey knew then that it would not be wise for him to remain and work in Jamaica beyond his three-year term.

Massey's term ended in 1966, and he and his wife returned to waiting responsibilities in Detroit. Although he stated to the Missionary Board that "the school will have become sufficiently established during our stay that its future could well be handled by other leaders," without his strong leadership and the necessary resources, the fortunes of Jamaica School of Theology deteriorated. Missionary George Buck continued to make efforts to implement aspects of the cooperative educational plan envisioned by Massey. In the end, however, the leaders of the Church of God in Jamaica decided against it. The Missionary Board became discouraged by the few students and the failure of the school to develop a cooperative relationship even with West Indies Bible Institute, a Church of God school which had been in existence in Trinidad since 1950. Consequently, without an adequate base of operation or a supporting cooperative relationship to broaden the base, Jamaica School of Theology closed its doors in 1970.

Since that fateful year, the Jamaican church has sorrowed over the loss of its school. The Missionary Board has sent scholarship assistance to help support selected persons seeking training. Local churches have relied on the leadership of ministers from the United States and Jamaicans with limited theological training, training gained earlier from the school that is no more or through Jamaica Theological Seminary in Kingston.

West Indies Theological College

The first reference to a pattern of theological education in the southern Caribbean was in 1922. Representatives from the Church of God in Barbados, British Guiana, and Trinidad and Tobago had begun meeting for a one-week period each year. A fixed period of each day was devoted to training leadership. There was serious reading and written examinations. The need was obvious, and this effort was at least a beginning.

During the lifetime of Jamaica School of Theology in the northern Caribbean, there was both the need and desire to begin a more formal, residential, educational work in the southern Caribbean. But the islands of this area were relatively small, scattered, and independent, presenting practical problems not experienced by the single, large island nation of Jamaica. Travel among the islands was inconvenient, costly, and complicated by immigration procedures and employment restriction on noncitizens. Nonetheless, the need for some means of training church leaders for the region was obvious, and the will of the churches and missionaries to do something became clear. The motivation was strengthened further in the 1940s by the rising demand for self-government and the corresponding need for the training of indigenous leadership.

In 1948 a plan for the possible beginning of a training program was proposed to the Missionary Board in Anderson, Indiana. Knowing the financial limitations of the Board, and concerned about the self-respect of those to be trained, the Claire Shultzes and Ralph Coolidges, American missionary couples who had arrived in 1945-46 in Trinidad and Tobago, proposed a self-help program. The Board approved, emphasizing that the project had to be self-supporting.

Soon $700 was raised by a challenge presented at the state youth camp in Pennsylvania. Tools were purchased and a shop was set up in a garage behind the mission residence at 15 Carlos Street in Port of Spain. With an offering from the church in Trinidad and Tobago for some working capital, the operation of the vocational department of the new West Indies Bible Institute began.

The first classes met in 1950 in the Sunday School rooms of the church down the street at 40 Carlos Street. There were nineteen part-time and seven full-time students, the latter including three from Trinidad and Tobago, two from Barbados, and one each from British Guiana and Grenada. The faculty were the Coolidges and Shultzes, and two members of the Port of Spain congregation, Carlton Cumberbatch who taught English, and Dr. Leopold Lynch who taught hygiene. Rev. Ralph Coolidge was the principal.

Claire Shultz later recalled that the subjects to be taught would be "about the same as those in the Theological Department of Anderson College or Pacific Bible College and would cover a period of four years." It was the substance of a two-year program spread over four years to accommodate the necessary work schedule of students. Typically students would attend classes several hours each day and work the rest of the day making coat hangers, ladders, ironing boards, and souvenirs for tourists.

Facilities soon were inadequate for the shop operation. Space for the materials and tools became a problem and the noise of the operation disturbed the quiet residential neighborhood. Something had to change. Then Wilbur Schield, friend of the Schultzes and businessman from Iowa, visited the operation during one of his business trips to South America. Challenged by the need and opportunity, he and his brother Vern gave $15,000 to help purchase a new site, five acres in the Santa Cruz valley some miles away over a nearby mountain. Here a small factory was built, more tools were provided, and a third missionary couple was made possible. The Oakley Millers came in 1952, she to teach and he, a woodworker, to staff the shop.

The first students of West Indies Bible Institute graduated in 1954. An all-purpose building and a small dormitory had been built by then, the shop was very active, and morale was high. Students were now coming from St. Kitts, Antigua, St. Vincent, and even Dutch-speaking Curacao and Spanish-speaking Panama and Costa Rica. Graduates began assuming leadership roles in the churches. Theodosia Francis (Cumberbatch), previously a young evangelist, became the pastor in San Fernando, Trinidad. Carlton Cumberbatch became a full-time teacher and later the president of the institute itself. Clifford Payne became pastor in Port of Spain, Trinidad, and Earl Proctor in Tobago, with others going to Barbados, Grenada, and Guiana.

Over the years, the shop operation was a blessing and a burden. It was promoted heavily in the churches, sometimes being referred to as "the sleeping giant" because it was seen as having great potential for generating funds for the school and the churches. It appeared essential for the viability of the academic program since most students had no other way to pay for their education. But conflict arose. While in Jamaica, the rapid growth of the secondary education department had threatened to overwhelm the theological education mission of Jamaica School of Theology, in Trinidad it was the vocational department. Particularly it was the view of the missionaries that the shop was too much of a competitor for the primary time and energy of students. On the other hand, many local church members felt that the shop's potential was being limited to the provision of student needs when it could and should have been further expanded to assist the churches also.

Donald and Betty Jo Johnson arrived as missionaries in 1956 to join the staff of the institute. As dean and then acting president, Donald Johnson helped bring into being an administrative reorganization which established a Board of Trustees representative of the Missionary Board and the churches in Barbados, Grenada, Guiana, and Trinidad and Tobago. The intent was to enable the local churches to assume more responsibility, partly through granting to the Board of Trustees the right to ratify officers of the institute appointed by the Missionary Board. Soon Carlton Cumberbatch, a local graduate of the institute, was appointed and ratified as the third president of WIBI, effective in June 1959. It was an historic year.

Another historic year was 1967 when President Cumberbatch graduated from Anderson College, the Oakley Millers ended their missionary service (the last missionaries assigned to the work of the institute), and WIBI graduate Clifford Payne was appointed dean, making the entire staff West Indian. Since then the Missionary Board has continued to invest substantial dollars in support of the operation of the institute rather than sending American personnel.

Payne was followed as dean in 1975 by another West Indian, Frank Drakes. By that silver anniversary year of WIBI's existence, forty-nine of its graduates had served as pastors, eleven as teachers in public or private schools, five as nurses, four as social workers, nine as Christian education workers, two as church leaders in ecumenical work, two as nursery and child care workers, three in secretarial work, and one in radio broadcasting. Over the years, several graduates have gone to England, Canada, or the United States as students in accredited colleges and universities and earned undergraduate and graduate degrees (including Anderson University in several cases).

In the 1970s the academic programs of WIBI included a two-year course of general preparation for the General Certificate of Education examinations and, built on that course with two additional years, a Ministerial Diploma course and a Christian Education Diploma course. An expansion in 1975 introduced a series of third and fourth year courses designed to assist selected students with the advanced-level General Certificate of Education examinations. Then in 1978 the institute's name was changed to West

Indies Theological College.

During these years, the dilemma of the shop continued and worsened. Finally the shop's operations failed altogether. There were business management problems, worker inefficiencies, and the increasing disrepair of equipment. The college, determined to keep this mainstay of student finances going, converted the shop into a commercial enterprise. But the dream of profits from this move never materialized. The new company, Masterbilt Products Limited, replaced the college's vocational department, finally started operations in 1972 after a delay, stopped functioning in 1974, and was liquidated in 1977—all without managing to contribute any revenue to the college's operations. This was indeed a depressing sequence of events.

Two major issues over the decades of the life of the college have had a major impact negatively on its development and are yet crucial to its future. One is its isolation and the other its accreditation.

In the late 1950s an experimental Caribbean ten-nation federation was launched and then failed. This was another evidence of the insular mentality and nationalism which have hindered regional progress in many ways. Jamaica, with its large Church of God population, went its own way. Any hope of a merger of the Church of God schools in Jamaica and Trinidad ended. Although each school was weak, there was no apparent way to cooperate for the good of both. Isolation prevailed.

But geography and politics were not the only isolating factors. Church identity inclined both schools not to become involved formally in a major ecumenical arrangement. The Jamaican school rejected such a possibility in the 1960s, and although WITC developed an informal relationship in 1985 with the nearby Caribbean Nazarene Theological College, nothing more has seemed feasible or desirable to either of the church constituencies involved. So WITC has remained largely a school of the south Caribbean only and of the Church of God only.

This isolation has been countered in part by the active involvement of WITC in the development of an interdenominational Caribbean association for theological education beginning in 1971. There also have been a few well-known educators from the American church who have taught for brief periods at the college, including Dr. Earl Martin in 1958, and Dr. and Mrs. John W. V.

Smith in 1984 (both from Anderson College). Also in 1984 an agreement was drawn with Warner Southern College in Florida that promised some practical help to the college and some of its students.

With such isolation and very limited financial resources, then, WITC has been poorly equipped to face the other challenge of needed accreditation. In its early years, WITC recruited many of the most gifted Church of God youth of the area. Despite its lack of institutional standing in the world of higher education, several of its graduates were able to excel because of their own ability and motivation. Over the years, however, educational aspirations and standards have risen sharply in the Caribbean. For the more gifted persons, education in the local university or abroad has become more feasible and popular, affecting adversely both the size and quality of WITC's student body and the focus of its educational programs. More of the students now attracted want preparation for the certificate exams on their way to "standard" higher education rather than only theological training for service specifically within the Church of God of the south Caribbean. In recent years, the student body has ranged from eight to twenty-five persons.

Presumably formal accreditation would help this circumstance and such an accrediting body has arisen. It is the Caribbean Evangelical Theological Association which works jointly with the American Association of Bible Colleges. WITC has had an active relationship with this association since its beginning in 1971, but has not been able to qualify for its accreditation. Without such and without a substantive ecumenical relationship or a major new source of support from within the Church of God, it became questionable in 1985 whether the college had a future. To date, for instance, nothing has ever replaced the supportive role played by the shop operation in the earlier years except for some direct support from the churches in the region and substantial dollar support from the Missionary Board in the United States.

In 1986 Dr. Barry Callen, Vice-President for Academic Affairs of Anderson College, visited the college to research its history and counsel with President Cumberbatch as he contemplated retirement after so many years with the school. Out of the resulting conversations came a call for a formal consultation of Caribbean leaders of the Church of God, the WITC Board of Trustees, a representative from the Missionary Board, and Dr. Callen as special resource person. An era seemed to be ending for the college and a new future had to be found.

The consultation convened on the campus in Trinidad on June 5-6, 1986. Ten countries were represented, including Jamaica. In 1985 the organization of the governance of WITC had been changed to extend the right of board membership to all of the countries associated with the Caribbean/Atlantic Assembly of the Church of God. This consultation began to demonstrate the widening circle of interest in and commitment to WITC.

Nine consensus statements were developed and agreed to by all participants as crucial guidelines for the future. They were:

1. It is affirmed by the Consultation members that the Church of God in the Caribbean needs a Church of God institution which seeks to prepare Christian leaders for service to the life of the Church of God in the Caribbean and to enable that church to fulfill its world mission.

2. Given the level of educational expectations in the Caribbean and the desire of the Consultation members to see provision for development of the best possible leadership for the church, every effort should be made to gain accreditation for this Church of God institution.

3. For this institution to be viable, the assemblies of the Church of God associated with the Caribbean/Atlantic Assembly must take increased responsibility for the necessary support of this institution and its students.

4. Since the leadership needs of the Church of God in the Caribbean are various, including traditional college education, extension education and the continuing education of ministers, this Church of God institution should be creative and flexible in its programming.

5. This Church of God institution, to become a reality, must be built within the limits of available resources and should take advantage of a foundation already laid. West Indies Theological College has laid such a foundation. It is the theological training institution currently recognized by the Caribbean/Atlantic Assembly of the Church of

God and affirmed by members of this Consultation as the proper place to begin.

6. The instructors at the West Indies Theological College should include representation from the entire Caribbean to the greatest extent possible. Their compensation should be at a level appropriate to their experience, their credentials, and the local cost of living.

7. The generation of adequate support for the operation of West Indies Theological College will require the development of some enterprise/plan which can produce income for the college in addition to church contributions.

8. Review should be made of the current nomination process for membership on the Board of Trustees of West Indies Theological College to ensure that the process is structured to bring to the Board the strongest potential membership. This review should include a reconsideration of the number, and the length of terms of service, of members of this Board.

9. The members of this Consultation have been informed about and heartily endorse the recent decision of the Board of Trustees to seek funding for the construction of an administration and academic building for West Indies Theological College.

As the many members left this consultation for their several home countries, the college still was small and struggling. But there was renewed hope that the college had a future. Some sense of direction had been achieved and a group commitment had been made. Within weeks the faculty proposed plans to offer the fourth year segment of the curriculum, thus hoping to implement the full four-year Bachelor of Theology program and work toward accreditation at that level. By 1988 there was government approval of plans for the new administration and academic building and fund raising for it among the Caribbean churches. These were steps of faith.

Edward Cumberbatch, who had come to Trinidad from Barbados in 1905, had been converted under the preaching of missionary George Pye and then ordained in 1913. He was the first West Indian ordained minister of the Church of God in Trinidad and in the entire southern Caribbean area. His son, Carlton, educated at

WITC and then Anderson College and its School of Theology, was the West Indian president of WITC from 1959 to 1988. He retired from the long tenure in that responsibility, being replaced by a native of Barbados, Martin Goodridge. This marked the end of an era; by faith it will be the beginning of another.

Table 11
West Indies Theological College
(Port of Spain, Trinidad)

Institutional Names:
   1950-1978 West Indies Bible Institute
   1978-   West Indies Theological College
Accreditations:
   None
Chief Executive Officers:
   1950-1956 Ralph Coolidge (principal)
   1956-1957 Claire Shultz (president)
   1957-1959 Donald Johnson (president)
   1959-1988 Carlton Cumberbatch (president)
   1988-   Martin Goodridge (president)
Chief Academic Officers:
   1950-1959 No One So Designated
   1959-1961 Donald Johnson
   1961-1964 Walter Lehmann
   1964-1967 No One So Designated
   1967-1974 Clifford Payne
   1974-1988 Frank Drakes
   1988-   Theodosia Cumberbatch
Current Chair of Governing Board:
   1984-   Hugh Drakes (St. Vincent)

Chapter 12
A Responsible Relationship Between Church and Colleges

The early period of pioneer activity in the Church of God had been characterized by a strong aversion to almost anything that resembled the organized life of the denominations. "Man-rule" in God's church was constantly identified as an evil to be shunned. Even in D. S. Warner's lifetime, however, it had become evident that "perhaps as much as 40 years more may elapse ere the Judge of all shall proclaim the end of time. . . ."[1] The urgency which had helped to fuel the fires of anti-institutionalism lessened somewhat by such a delay in the Lord's return. Even some long-range planning slowly came to be seen as justifiable.

Some Beginning Guidelines

In the decades that followed the death of Warner in 1895 the concern for the effectiveness of evangelistic outreach and the stewardship of available resources necessarily led the young Church of God movement to certain adjustments in its initial anti-organizational stance. By 1898, for instance, the growing demand for "pure literature" had brought the prayerful conclusion that "God has moved that the publishing work be placed upon a firmer basis by the formation of a stock company, under the laws of the state of West Virginia."[2]

Increasingly congregations were becoming local property owners with residential pastors, something which D. S. Warner once had seen as "a snare to entangle God's flying messengers."[3] Missionary activity broadened across the world, sometimes in such a haphazard way that the Ministerial Assembly in 1909 chose seven brethren as a missionary committee with the duty of "advising, instructing, encouraging, or restraining those who feel called to the foreign missionary field."[4] The General Ministerial Assembly of the Church of God was itself formalized at the Anderson Camp Meeting of 1917, partly to increase participation in cooperative ministries and partly to give general direction to the business of the church. It was becoming obvious to most thoughtful people that the urgent work of the Lord needed some careful coordination and even regulation so that it could be implemented effectively over an extended period of years in a highly organized society.

With this new understanding came the founding of such program agencies as the Board of Church Extension and Home Missions (1920) and the Board of Christian Education (1923). By 1928 it had become so apparent that these agencies needed to have their separate fund raising efforts coordinated that the General Ministerial Assembly established the Associated Budgets. Not long after came additional steps of coordination which eventually evolved into the present Executive Council of the Church of God, a separately incorporated body which coordinates the budget askings of all general agencies and the long-range planning of these cooperative ministries.

This pattern of institutional development was the result of concerned responses to obvious needs in the life of the church. It evolved slowly and sometimes with a bad conscience in the face of the early reaction against nearly all forms of typical denominational life. Speaking sociologically, the Church of God might be seen as having passed through several standard phases, arriving only after decades of ministry to a "sophistication" level which would encourage the establishment of institutions, including institutions of higher education, and which finally would create the need to formalize the coordination of their many activities.[5]

As early as 1918, with Spokane Bible School, Kansas City Bible School, and Anderson Bible Training School in existence, there already was some need to discuss the most appropriate relationship among the schools developing within the boundaries of the Church of God. The General Ministerial Assembly of 1918 addressed this need and appointed D. O. Teasley, J. W. Phelps, R. L. Berry, A. F. Gray, and R. H. Owens to comprise a committee that would explore "the school question." As A. F. Gray later recalled, the committee's discussion involved some significant disagreement.

> As the Spokane school was so far away it would be expected to draw students and support from its own territory. The Kansas City school was expected, so someone thought, to draw its students and support chiefly from Missouri, whereas the Anderson school would serve the church in general and be entitled to general support. Brother Berry opposed this conclusion vigorously. He declared the Kansas City school benefited the whole church and if it was not entitled to general support neither was Anderson. He said that Missouri could support the Kansas City school by itself, if need be, but this would lessen its giving to other causes.[6]

Finally the committee concluded that any work of a general nature was entitled to general support—and apparently all existing schools thought of themselves as "general" in nature and came to be recognized as such. The General Ministerial Assembly then proceeded to pass a resolution creating an "Education Fund" to be held by the Missionary Board of the Church of God and distributed "to the existing Bible training schools in proportion to the number of enrolled students."[7]

Here was the earliest attempt on record to muster general church support for institutions of higher education and to set some precedent for how the evolving schools should be interrelated and funded by the church. As Brother Berry had argued for the national status of Kansas City Bible School (and thus no regional limitation on its recruitment or fund raising boundaries), so did the managing committee of Anderson Bible Training School (later Anderson University) in regard to its own prerogatives. Its minutes of September 19, 1921, stated "that we should not be barred out of the territory west of the Mississippi River in soliciting school funds."

Clearly each school saw itself as serving the whole church and was opposed to the imposition of a system of limitations. Some general coordination and certainly widespread support were seen as desirable by the schools and the church. However, centralized control of the several institutions was judged inappropriate.

Steps Toward a Permanent Commission

And so it went through the next two decades. Schools were founded and died with little church-wide consultation and virtually no conscious coordination and certainly no centralized control. An ambitious venture like Warner Memorial University in Texas (1929-1933), for instance, had been justified by area ministers as a regionally necessary enterprise, but its demise was hurtful financially to many persons across the United States who had invested in it. There was the inevitable afterthought—was it a legitimate venture for the church, short-lived only because of the Great Depression, or was it the unexamined and unchecked dream of one man? Would it ever have come into being if there had been some formal means of coordinating the church's total investment in higher education?

A young minister named Mack Caldwell, a graduate of Anderson Bible Training School and dean of Southern Bible Institute in Georgia (another educational dream that survived for only two years in the mid-1920s), became acquainted with the systematic way the Church of the Nazarene was handling its institutions of higher education. While a student and teacher at Trevecca College in Nashville, Tennessee, from 1928-1930, Rev. Caldwell learned that the Church of the Nazarene had established a General Board of Education. By 1919 it also had issued a document explaining a system of "educational zones" within the church, each designed to support only one college within its bounds, with no college making systematic efforts to raise funds or recruit students outside its own zone. In contrast, Caldwell observed that the Church of God was going about this business very inefficiently, with things too centralized in the Midwest. Being a dreamer and activist himself, he began to seek ways to do something about this concern.

The years during and immediately after World War II brought increasing unrest in the Church of God. There was a considerable amount of independent action. The scene was crisscrossed by the proliferation of church-related programs being started by individuals or groups. Often activities were competitive and wholly uncoordinated. Being understood as Spirit-inspired ventures in a Spirit-led church, they generally hoped to draw upon the resources of the whole church. Rumors were abroad that more new schools were on regional or even local drawing boards.

The vast majority of pastors in those years were not college trained and had few resources to support expensive programs of continuing education. So a minister in Oklahoma, Rev. Horace Hathcoat, began offering ministerial degrees by correspondence (Berean Bible College). The national Board of Christian Education also saw the need and on September 12, 1945, its Executive Committee issued the following directive:

> To meet the rising need and demand on the part of pastors for courses they can study individually at home, the secretary [T. Franklin Miller] was instructed to explore the possibilities of promoting our second series leadership training courses for the study of ministers.

Dr. Otto F. Linn, former Bible professor at Anderson College (University), became Dean of Pacific Bible College (Warner Pacific) in Portland in 1942. In June 1944 he found himself before the annual meeting of the national Board of Christian Education presenting a case for the establishment of an "educational commission to study the field of higher education in the Church of God and to discourage many of the attempts in the field." The Board agreed with Linn and, according to its minutes of June 16, 1944, decided to appoint two board members to meet with the presidents of Anderson College, Pacific Bible College, and Alberta Bible Institute (Gardner Bible College) "to consider the possibility of setting up such an advisory committee on higher education." E. E. Perry and Walter S. Haldeman were so named.

Each June between 1945 and 1948 an ad hoc group of concerned ministers met "under the trees" at Anderson Camp Meeting. T. Franklin Miller agreed to be the secretary because he was the only one in the group who had access to a general agency office and could provide some clerical support. He recalls that Mack Caldwell continued as a "moving force" in this group. A. Leland Forrest and John W. V. Smith were in the earliest conversations, but soon they were joined by men like A. T. Rowe, John A. Morrison, and William E. Reed. In a letter on March 7, 1979, John Smith recalled what prompted their concern:

> Several sections of the country were discussing the possibility of launching new institutions. Ever since the failure of Warner Memorial University at Eastland, Texas, there had been repeated expressed interest in starting another school in the South Central Plains area. Specific sites had already been proposed in Texas, Oklahoma, and Kansas for the opening of such a school. There was also some preliminary discussion in the wind about a school in Southern California, a discussion which eventuated in the founding of Arlington College a few years later. There was also a considerable interest in getting a college started in the Southeastern states with some proposals for specific locations. There were likewise rumors to the effect that Pacific Bible College was going to ask for participation in the World Service Budget and that possibly they would be expanding their program to offer a full three-year seminary course above the college degrees they were already offering. Dr. Otto Linn had stated this dream on many occasions.

William E. Reed, in a letter dated February 5, 1979, also recalled that Horace Hathcoat was strongly promoting a correspondence school education for ministers. "Some of us did not want to give any encouragement to that type of development."

The talking finally turned to action in 1948. In an attempt to stimulate discussion and precipitate some action by the General Ministerial Assembly, a petition was drawn up and circulated on the Anderson Camp Meeting grounds among persons known to be concerned about such issues. Thirty-six ministers attached their names to the petition, including Maurice Berquist, Mack Caldwell, Charlie Cheeks, I. K. Dawson, Harry L. Harp, William E. Reed, Herschell and Hillery Rice, Warren C. Roark, John W. V. Smith, and E. E. Wolfram. It is probably significant that most of the signers were not from the educational "establishment." The concern was deep and from across the church. In the form of this petition, the concern found its way to the agenda of the 1948 General Ministerial Assembly.

The petition received formal attention in the morning session of June 16. It was adopted in principle by a voice vote, with the chair of the assembly being instructed to proceed in the naming of members to the new commission. The petition read:

> We, the undersigned, petition the business committee to bring before the General Ministerial Assembly the question of setting up an educational commission of 15 or more members, two-thirds of whom shall not be officially connected with present institutions of higher learning. The purpose of this educational commission to be: 1. To survey the needs and resources for higher education in the Church of God; and 2. To plan an adequate national program of higher education. The findings and suggestions of which commission shall be presented to the General Ministerial Assembly.

And so it began. There was a sense of needing to pull together in a time when fragmentation seemed to be everywhere. In this same assembly, for instance, the Committee on Revision and Planning reported progress in its work "towards more satisfactory methods of nominations to the boards, more direct control of the boards by the ministers, and toward a more representative ministerial assembly."[8] A few weeks later R. L. Berry announced in the August 21, 1948, issue of the *Gospel Trumpet* that "unity of action is imperative." He insisted that showing "the most hearty loyalty to the Church of God world program" is essential if the Church of God is to make an impact on the needs of the world. Keenly aware of the independent and critical attitude of some, he concluded somewhat scoldingly:

> Are some of us wanting to be dictators? Do we want things to go just as we think best? Is our judgment so perfect that we throw over a church program because we think some things could be better? Let us analyze our minds and hearts in this matter, lest we be found dictators in heart, persons who will not play at all unless the Church plays as we want it to.

That 1948 General Ministerial Assembly had been especially active. It authorized the preparation of a manual on ministerial ordination in the hope of making more uniform the procedures used across the country. It adopted a pension plan for ministers, something that had been discussed for twenty years. And it adopted a record-breaking budget totaling $785,000, with higher education represented by amounts of $126,650 to Anderson College and $50,700 to Pacific Bible College (a total of 22.59 percent of the budget devoted to higher education). It had also taken the first small step in attempting to bring some conscious coordination to the higher education enterprises of the Church of God.

The "commission" on higher education, authorized for a three-year period by the 1948 General Ministerial Assembly, was chaired initially by Mack Caldwell. At the end of this initial period its life was extended by one year at the request of the commission itself. When the extension expired in June 1952, a Study Committee on Christian Education was appointed to serve for three years. In May of 1953 this study committee elected as its officers Adam W. Miller, chair; Samuel C. Sharp, vice-chair; and T. Franklin Miller, secretary.

Exploration and Frustration

These early years might best be described as ones of general exploration and philosophical frustration. First the exploration.

A series of preliminary surveys were conducted by the new committee because it was evident that so little was actually known about so many significant matters. These surveys were reported in 1950 as revealing:

1. That there is an undetermined number of our young people who are entering college each year, only a small percentage of whom attend Church of God schools. A more complete survey for ascertaining the accurate number and vocation of these students is necessary for further guidance in reaching them.
2. There is considerable sentiment in certain areas in favor of establishing new schools in those areas. As yet there has been no adequate study for determining the specific educational needs of each area.
3. We have an indication that there are . . . qualified

teachers for the college level whose services are not being used in Church of God institutions and there is a growing number of people now in training for teaching on the college level. The exact number and qualifications of most of these prospective teachers is not yet known.

It was concluded that "a definite program for providing adequate opportunity for training and a system of maintaining contact with the young people should be inaugurated." Otherwise, it was feared, the church likely would lose many of its youth.

With this exploration of the issues came the philosophical frustration. Exactly what was the status and future of this study committee and what was and should it be empowered to do about anything it discovered? How much regulation of higher education was needed and could be justified?

The study committee started right off in 1949 by aggressively putting before the General Ministerial Assembly, and having accepted by the Assembly, these substantive guidelines:

1. We recommend that the General Ministerial Assembly go on record as discouraging the practice of our ministers either granting or receiving theological or academic degrees given solely on correspondence work. However, we do not wish to see the General Ministerial Assembly discouraging home study courses and reading courses not offered for degrees.

2. We recommend to the General Ministerial Assembly that, for the sake of coordinating the educational work of the church, individuals or groups desiring to establish institutions of higher learning seek the counsel of and avail themselves of the resources of the Commission on Higher Education of the General Ministerial Assembly.

3. We recommend to the General Ministerial Assembly that all ministers be encouraged to avail themselves of the existing avenues of furthering the education of ministers and lay leaders, such as ministers' institutes, first, second and third series courses offered through the Board of Christian Education, study courses at camp meetings, etc.

4. We recommend to the General Ministerial Assembly that it urge pastors who live near institutions of higher

learning to make and maintain contact with Church of God students in these schools either through a campus fellowship group or by integrating them into the local church youth fellowship.

Again in 1952, when it was making its case for a new three-year lease on life to continue its exploratory work, the study committee argued openly that "before any constructive planning can be done, before the structuring of a total educational program in the church can be accomplished, an intensive study and survey of the whole church ought to be made. . . ." In view was a "resultant structuring of a total educational program" in which the study committee would serve as follows:

1. Be the medium through which the faculty of the various colleges or seminaries are interchanged, library books are shared, and other services of mutual benefit are shared, such as assisting one another in dealing with accrediting agencies, sharing findings of faculty committees and other academic matters;

2. Be the sponsoring agent in keeping contact between the student bodies of the various schools;

3. Define spheres of activity, of enlistment, of student fieldwork, of financial appeal, and other activities carried on by the colleges;

4. Give counsel and guidance to brethren who contemplate the establishment of institutions of higher learning;

5. Act as the medium through which the interaction between the actual pastoral, teaching, and missionary situations, and the training given for each, is registered, studied, and recommendations made to colleges concerning curriculum, equipment, and procedure;

6. Be alert to areas of duplication or neglect and report any of such to the colleges;

7. Stimulate the colleges to aggressive efforts to provide guidance, incentive, and information to local pastors, state and district Christian education and youth leaders, in the enlistment of our youth for service needing college and seminary training, and to act as a coordinator of these promotional and recruiting activities;

8. Make available to the various educational institutions of the church, on the basis of careful study, certain necessary information and shared experience pertinent to the establishing of theological seminaries of graduate study, colleges, or Bible schools.

By 1952 membership of the study committee had come to include Mack Caldwell, Ronald Joiner, John W. V. Smith, Ida Byrd Rowe, T. Franklin Miller, and Carl Kardatzke. These persons saw a big need that could be met only with coordinated action. But they were only a temporary study committee supposed to be exploring, among other things, the need for a permanent body. And given the nonauthoritarian nature of the general work of the Church of God, the rather independent free-church mentality, the regionalism, and the autonomous nature of institutions of higher education within the church, the chances of successfully introducing a church-wide and carefully structured and controlled educational plan were not good. In fact, the several functions which the study committee projected for itself in 1952 (listed above) were very aspirational indeed given the magnitude of the problems and the inherent limitations of a tradition strongly opposed to "man-rule" in the life of the church.

The need was real and the persons involved were determined. In June 1953 the General Ministerial Assembly received the following report:

> The present thinking of the committee is that such a commission should think of itself as an agency of the church rather than as an agency of educational institutions, and must have sufficient authority to carry out its functions. Such a commission should think of itself as a planning commission for the educational program of the church and, as such, ought to develop the long-range program of educational development.

While the commission was announcing that it should be established "as an authoritative body," it also was conceding that "maintaining the true cooperation of the several institutions of higher education must be by request and consent and any benefits or penalties for cooperative endeavor or refusal of such be referred to the Assembly for action."

As stated in its June 1953 report to the Assembly, the suggested goal was to balance the privilege of being a recognized center of planning and coordination and the limitation of being such only "in terms of fraternal guidance" without attempting "to legislate or enforce any rule upon the institution." Commission members now included institutional representatives Milo L. Chapman (Pacific Bible College); John A. Morrison (Anderson College); Adam W. Miller (School of Theology); Gordon Schieck (Alberta Bible Institute); and T. Franklin Miller (Board of Christian Education). Members appointed in 1953 by the assembly chair were Harry L. Harp, James Wade, W. I. Plough, Samuel C. Sharp, and Harold Boyer.

The Final Step to Permanence

In 1954 the Association of the Churches of God in Southern California announced the decision to establish a four-year Bible college in southern California, with the doors to open in the fall of 1954. In a resolution directed to the 1954 General Ministerial Assembly, the association defended its move. It stated that southern California was an ideal location for a school, that students in the Los Angeles area likely would not go to Anderson College, Pacific Bible College, or South Texas Bible Institute because of the distance and that the churches of southern California "have repeatedly expressed their eagerness to operate within the framework of the general agencies of the church." This resolution, submitted by C. H. Joiner and A. J. Kempin as officers of the association, was received by the assembly and apparently shifted to the future agenda of the commission for discussion.

By June of 1954 the commission had developed a statement of "recommended criteria for the establishment of institutions of higher education" (see Appendix A). It reported to the assembly that year that these criteria had formed the basis for consultation with representatives from the southeastern states, World Evangelism Institute, Arlington College of Southern California, Gulf-Coast Bible College of Houston, Texas, and Kansas. As usual, the report concluded by noting that the "high interest evidenced in the establishment of institutions of higher education would seem to indicate the desirability of a strong, permanent Commission on Higher Education."

The California development helped spark even more concern that the commission was needed permanently. In successfully proposing to the 1955 General Ministerial Assembly a three-year extension of its life, the commission argued:

> As educational institutions grow they come to find that the sectional and regional support which once maintained them is no longer sufficient and, in view of the service they render to the church at large, these educational institutions would naturally look to the church at large for financial support. This fact further underscores for us the need for a permanent Commission, not only to serve in a coordinating capacity, but which will also be prepared to advise and counsel with such groups as contemplate setting up additional institutions of education. Such services rendered by the Commission would enable us to avoid setting up more institutions than the church could adequately maintain.

Finally, in 1957, the commission came forward with a formal proposal for its own existence on a permanent basis, by-laws and all. When the discussion died away, it seemed best for the ministers to think about it for a year. Then on June 17, 1958, the issue was taken from the table and passed. After a decade of exploratory activity it was ordered by the General Ministerial Assembly that the commission be a standing body within the Church of God and that the commission be charged with the following responsibilities:

> 1. To awaken the entire church to the conviction that true religion and true education complement each other, and that education highly conceived is Christian education, and that the promotion of Christian higher education is a proper activity of the church;
> 2. To lay plans for and to guide the development of the total higher education program of the church;
> 3. To establish and recommend criteria for the development of institutions of higher education in the Church of God;
> 4. To act as a connection link between the institutions and the church, urging the church to help the schools, and

helping the schools to better serve the church;

5. To arrange for coordination in the promotional and recruiting activities of the existing institutions;

6. To assist the church in the fullest possible use of her talent in the educational and training program of the church;

7. To carry on research and study to make available to the church educational information;

8. To cooperate whenever feasible and desirable with other commissions on Christian higher education.

Now the commission existed on a firm and long-term basis. It was hoped that it could bring effective coordination even though it lacked authoritative powers over the institutions involved. Within this framework the exploratory period was over and the real work was to begin.

Work of the Commission

Table 12 reports the leadership of the commission since its formal establishment. Obviously many significant leaders within the Church of God and its institutions of higher education have been very involved in the work of the commission. Given the stated purposes for its existence, the commission has functioned from year to year in a very central and changing and sometimes troubled arena of the church's life. There has been a constant mixture of aspiration, accomplishment, and frustration.

It became the commission's annual practice to receive and review reports from the several colleges, the School of Theology, and the national Board of Christian Education. Those reports have contained information about each school's enrollment, personnel, finances, programs, and facilities. In addition the commission has addressed a wide range of important matters of common concern to these schools, including their nature, existence, funding, programs, and relationships to each other, to the Church of God, and to the larger community of higher education. A chronological listing (1970 to the present) of major agenda items is found in Table 13. This listing highlights the range of issues addressed and challenges faced.

To Facilitate or Control?

A review of these years of commission activity demonstrates the obvious need for such a body and stimulates appreciation for the seriousness with which the commission has approached its tasks. Throughout, however, there has been a dilemma. There is no doubt that the commission has played important roles and been influential at several crucial points; but those roles and that influence have been contained within a rather narrowly prescribed framework. As T. Franklin Miller stated it in a taped interview in January 1980, the big issue has always been a philosophical one. Do we want in the Church of God a body that will "facilitate conversation" or one that has power and authority over existing and new institutions. The frustration has come, he noted, from the limitations of the obvious choice of facilitator. It probably is the inevitable impasse given the church's approach to organization and Holy Spirit leadership. Institutional anarchy, Miller concluded, is the risk we have chosen rather than the risks inherent in becoming burdened with the creation of standard denominational machinery.

This facilitator role has been meaningful and very much worthwhile, as a review of the commission agendas clearly shows. But the felt need for more coordination and even some control in the church's higher education efforts has been voiced often. In taped interviews in 1980, Milo Chapman and Fred Shackleton, each with long-term involvement in Church of God higher education, expressed this felt need. According to Shackleton, "the total enterprise of higher education in the Church of God would have been much stronger if from the beginning a total plan could have been developed that had the official approval and support of the church at large." Chapman observed that the church has needed "responsible leadership" in higher education, but instead "we formed a discussion group with little power to act. We talk mostly at superficial levels and do not try to formulate policy for higher education in the church."

Mack Caldwell, very influential in the beginnings of the commission, shared a similar perspective with me in a 1979 taped interview. He saw real need for a strengthening of the commission.

"We need the commission now even more than earlier in our history." Why? He thought that there was an inequitable distribution of funds, too much power lying with the larger institutions, too much vested interest resident in the commission's membership, and too little church control over the whole scene. "Instead of the church running its colleges," he concluded, "the colleges are running the church!"

Such concerns, plus events in the early part of the 1980s, set the stage for another extensive reconsideration of the composition and work of the commission.

A New Beginning

In the 1980 General Assembly sessions in Anderson there was sharp criticism by some ministers of a particular set of curricular and instructional circumstances at Anderson College. This public criticism dramatized an apparently deep and dangerous division on a series of issues church-wide and introduced a difficult and volatile year. As one way of helping, the Board of Directors of the Executive Council convened in January 1981 a "dialogue on internal unity." Some thirty church leaders from across the country met and decided that the issue of biblical authority was probably the most central issue to be discussed. These leaders came to consensus on a set of affirmations on this issue and proceeded to make recommendations in other areas of prominent concern. One recommendation was the following:

> A serious concern is expressed that our colleges are essentially unrelated and competitive. Some initiative should be taken to speak to this major problem.

By the General Assembly of June 1981 the Board of Trustees of Anderson College had prepared a major report in response to the issues which had emerged in the General Assembly the year before. Beyond speaking to issues related particularly to Anderson College, the report identified "two major and yet unresolved concerns which . . . deserve responsible and church-wide attention." One of these, the relationship of the church to its colleges, read:

> Historically, the relationship of the Church of God to its colleges has been largely informal and undefined. There

has been the relationship created by the election of trustees, the ratification of chief executive officers, budgetary support and general reporting. However, there is little clarity regarding the church's expectations of its colleges, and there has not been a widespread understanding of what constitutes a responsible relationship between a church body and its institutions of higher learning. We urge an exploration of this subject.

In December 1981 a second dialogue on internal unity was convened with a new group of thirty church leaders from across the nation chosen by the Executive Council office. Again the issue of higher education was singled out by the group for attention. This group reported "a great deal of frustration . . . over the competition and independency of action on the part of our educational institutions and other problems relating to the need for overall coordination and supervision of our higher educational process." They recommended a study of how other church bodies handle these things and then called for some action "for the corporate structuring of our approach to higher education."

This recommendation was received and then forwarded by the Executive Council to the Commission on Christian Higher Education. In January 1983 the commission considered the matter and decided on a path of action. It called for a meeting of the presidents, deans, and board chairs of the schools in the United States which were predominantely maintained and governed by the Church of God (Anderson University, with its School of Theology, Bay Ridge Christian College, Mid-America Bible College, Warner Pacific College and Warner Southern College). The purpose was to "initiate candid conversation regarding the overarching goal of serving and advancing the Church of God through its ministries of higher education and to work deliberately at enhancing that which is mutually supportive and minimizing that which is combative." This group met in Kansas City, Missouri, on November 10-11, 1983, established its own agenda, experienced candid and fruitful conversations, judged the meeting to have been historic and most wise, and established a possible agenda for a second such meeting. One item on that agenda was clarification of the possible future role of this ad hoc group in relation to the Commission on Christian Higher Education.

By this time many straws of change were blowing in the wind. The Division of World Service joined the process by evolving a "higher education scenario" in a brainstorming session during its 1984 spring meeting. Concerns about general church budgeting and fund raising, of course, made up the immediate context. This scenario was sent by the Executive Council office to college boards of trustees for review and reaction. Partly because the scenario called for a "board of regents" with governance functions over the colleges and a regional concept for college fund raising, reaction was negative. In part, the December 10, 1984, response of the Anderson College Board of Trustees was:

> 1. The scenario takes for granted that the problems likely to arise in the more centralized system proposed . . . are preferable to the present problems. This may not be the case.
> 2. The scenario appears to move in a direction counter to a central characteristic of the heritage of the Church of God, i.e., a resistance to centralizing power and authority in human hands.
> 3. The concept of "regionalism" is unacceptable to colleges which, by tradition and mission, serve the national church.

Apparently, the scenario was destined to play only one role, that of stimulating more exploration.

Where, then, would a new beginning come from? If not this more centralized approach, then what? The answer was to come initially from the proposed second meeting of the presidents, deans, and board chairs, this time on November 29-30, 1984 at the site of the new Mid-America Bible College campus under construction in Oklahoma City, Oklahoma. It was agreed by this significant group of leaders in Church of God higher education that the following assumptions were significant considerations in any recommendations for change:

> 1. As servants of the Church, the colleges should be responsive to the evolving needs within the Church and society.

2. The Church deserves proper accountability from the colleges it supports.
3. The diversity among our colleges is real and valued, and healthy forms of competition are appropriate and effective.
4. There is need for raising awareness about the value of Christian Higher Education within the Church; there will be long-term deterioration of the Church if increasing numbers of students are educated in institutions other than our own.
5. The present loose affiliation of colleges lacks the means to effectively guide and promote the cause of Christian Higher Education within the Church.
6. The financial needs of Church of God colleges will continue to outpace the growth of World Service resources in basic budget through the end of this century.
7. The pool of prospective traditional students is shrinking and Church of God colleges are presently attracting only a small percentage of these, even though these colleges have the capacity to serve a greater number.
8. Financial support for private education from non-church sources is likely to decrease.
9. The character of Christian Higher Education is being endangered through legal challenges and the imposition of external criteria.

With these considerations in mind and remembering the value experienced in the two meetings, the group developed and proposed a model for reconstituting the membership of the commission. The basic idea was for the commission to be this ad hoc group plus a few at-large members elected by the General Assembly. It was thought that such a model would strengthen the commission without adding the negatives of centralized control over sovereign college corporations.

This model was reviewed by the commission in January 1985 and, with only slight modification, was forwarded to and approved by the Executive Council in May and the General Assembly in June. Therefore, beginning July 1, 1985, the commission was enlarged to comprise twenty-eight members, including the "key decision makers in higher education." This had finally been determined to be the best way to "further facilitate cooperative efforts while minimizing unwholesome competitive activities." The new membership now included:

Anderson University president, dean, and board chair	3
Warner Pacific College president, dean, and board chair	3
Mid-America Bible College president, dean, and board chair	3
Bay Ridge Christian College president, dean, and board chair	3
Warner Southern College president, dean, and board chair	3
Anderson University School of Theology dean	1
Azusa Pacific University president	1
Executive Council representative (staff director)	1
Elected representatives (General Assembly)	6
Board of Christian Education executive secretary	1
Gardner Bible College president, dean, and board chair	3
Total	28

Looking Back for Perspective

Annually the commission has sought to be a constructive force on behalf of the whole enterprise of higher education. One means of accomplishing this goal has been the addressing of pressing issues. Another has been the collecting of comparative information from the institutions. Following is a series of tables highlighting the leadership of the commission, the issues addressed, and some of the information gathered. Several observations on trends seen in this information are included in Chapter 13.

Notes:

[1] *Gospel Trumpet,* January 3, 1895.
[2] *Gospel Trumpet,* October 13, 1898, p. 4.
[3] *Gospel Trumpet,* March 10, 1892.
[4] F. G. Smith, *Look on the Fields* (Anderson, Indiana: Missionary Board of the Church of God, 1920).
[5] See Val Clear, *Where the Saints Have Trod* (Chesterfield, Ind.: Midwest Publications, 1977).
[6] A. F. Gray, *Time and Tides* (Autobiography published privately, 1966?), p. 91
[7] *Gospel Trumpet,* July 4, 1918, p. 4.
[8] *Gospel Trumpet,* July 24, 1948, p. 19.

Table 12
Officers: Commission on Christian Higher Education of the Church of God

	Chair	**Vice-Chair**	**Secretary**
1958	Wade, J.	Martin, E.	Sharp, S.
1959	Wade, J.	Nicholson, R.	Sharp, S.
1960	Wade, J.	Nicholson, R.	Sharp, S.
1961	Wade, J.	Nicholson, R.	Sharp, S.
1962	Wade, J.	Nicholson, R.	Sharp, S.
1963	Nicholson, R.	Massey, J.	Baker, M.
1964	Nicholson, R.	Massey, J.	Baker, M.
1965	Nicholson, R.	Miller, T. F.	Baker, M.
1966	Nicholson, R.	Miller, T. F.	Thor, J. C.
1967	Nicholson, R.	Lindemuth, M.	Thor, J. C.
1968	Nicholson, R.	Lindemuth, M.	Thor, J. C.
1969	Massey, J.	Nicholson, R.	Sharpe, H.
1970	Massey, J.	Nicholson, R.	Sharpe, H.
1971	Massey, J.	Nicholson, R.	Sharpe, H.
1972	Chapman, M.	Nicholson, R.	Sharpe, H.
1973	Chapman, M.	Nicholson, R.	Sharpe, H.
1974	Chapman, M.	Nicholson, R.	Sharpe, H.
1975	Chapman, M.	Nicholson, R.	Sharpe, H.
1976	Chapman, M.	Nicholson, R.	Sharpe, H.
1977	Chapman, M.	Nicholson, R.	Sharpe, H.
1978	Chapman, M.	Nicholson, R.	Sharpe, H.
1979	Menchinger, F.	Nicholson, R.	Sharpe, H.
1980	Menchinger, F.	Nicholson, R.	Sharpe, H.
1981	Menchinger, F.	Nicholson, R.	Sharpe, H.
1982	Menchinger, F.	Nicholson, R.	Sharpe, H.
1983	Nicholson, R. (acting)	Nicholson, R.	Sharpe, H.
1984	Nicholson, R.	Malbone, T.	Sharpe, H.
1985	Courtney, D.	Malbone, T.	Sharpe, H.
1986	Courtney, D.	Malbone, T.	Grubbs, J.
1987	Malbone, T.	Beach, V.	Grubbs, J.
1988	Malbone, T.	Beach, V.	Grubbs, J.
1989	Malbone, T.	Beach, V.	Callen, B.

These officers have comprised the executive committee of the commission and as such have sought to give guidance to the work of the commission.

Table 13
Record of Central Agenda Items Commission on Christian Higher Education of the Church of God

Annually the commission receives and reviews reports from the several colleges and the School of Theology of the church. These reports contain information about the school's enrollments, personnel, programs, and facilities. In addition, the commission addresses important matters of common concern to these schools and their relationships to the life and ministries of the Church of God. Found below is a dated listing of some of these common concerns and actions.

1970 Addressed the question of institutional membership in the commission. How was the commission to relate to the colleges not fitting into the pattern used for membership (Azusa Pacific, Bay Ridge, Gardner, and Warner Southern Colleges)?

1971 Report of the commission's study of college attendance patterns of Church of God high school graduates (1969 data).

1972 Attempted to draft a common philosophy of Christian higher education which might serve a unifying purpose among all Church of God related schools of higher education.

1973 Reported the preliminary and foundational steps taken to fulfill the commission's assignment, voted by the General Assembly in 1972, to study theological education and ministerial training in the Church of God.

1974 Reported progress on the commission's study of theological education and ministerial training in the Church of God.

1975 Continued work on the commission's study of theological education and ministerial training in the Church of God.

1976 Completed and reported to the General Assembly the findings and recommendations emerging from its study of theological education and ministerial training in the

Church of God. Continued a study of the best way to train Black leaders for service to the church in the South (assignment from the 1975 General Assembly in response to the request for general agency status by Bay Ridge Christian College).

1977 Final report and commission recommendations regarding the training of Black leaders for service to the church in the South, including the establishment of a fund for Black ministerial education.

1978 Reviewed the initial attempts to generate church support for the fund for Black ministerial education. Established a policy for administering available funds for Black ministerial students. Reviewed the expenditure of available funds by Bay Ridge Christian College and the Center for Pastoral Studies of Anderson School of Theology.

1979 Studied ways to keep the cause of Christian higher education before the church. Reviewed funds received and expended for Black ministerial education. Gave attention to the critical circumstances being experienced by Warner Pacific College.

1980 Sought ways to communicate to the church and individual families the importance of Christian higher education. Reported significant involvement with the National Congress of Church Related Colleges and Universities. Reported on the commission's 1979 study of college attendance patterns of Church of God young people. (See Chapter 13, point 12.)

1981 Reported on its study, evaluation, and recommendations related to the Black ministerial education fund. Established an information file for prospective faculty members for the colleges of the church.

1982 Attention given to the impact of government funding programs for higher education, the negative potential for church-related higher education of litigation in progress and the interrelationships of the several colleges of the Church of God.

1983 To serve the best interests of all the church's colleges, the commission worked to convene a meeting of the presidents, deans, and board chairs of the colleges predominately governed by the Church of God, to develop a brochure highlighting all of the Church of God colleges, and to assist the colleges in securing the names of Church of God high school juniors and seniors.

1984 Convened a meeting of the president, dean, and board chair of each college related predominantly to the Church of God in the United States (Kansas City, November 1983). Solicited from pastors the names of high school juniors and seniors for the use of the colleges. Initiated publishing of a brochure highlighting all of the colleges.

1985 Reviewed a proposed new structure for the commission coming from the meeting of presidents/deans/board chairs and another developed within the Division of World Service. Considered current trends in higher education. Received study of the formal ways the colleges are related to the Church of God.

1986 Convened on the new campus of Mid-America Bible College. Met for the first time as newly constituted by the General Assembly. Experienced enthusiasm for the potential of an increasingly effective commission. Action taken requesting alteration for the agency colleges of the 1985 General Assembly action limiting the tenure of board members. Discussion of the proper role of the commission in regard to higher education worldwide in the Church of God.

1987 Hosted by Warner Pacific College in Portland. Asked each elected member (not representing an institution) to react candidly to the issues seen in the institutional reports. Presidents, deans, board chairs, and elected members began annual practice of meeting in one session as separate groups, then reporting to the whole commission. Reviewed "university" question for Anderson College and the continuing financial crisis at Mid-America Bible College (failure to sell the Texas property). Attention given to a proposed updated statement of the purpose and functions of the commission.

1988 Called for a repeat of the study done twice before of the current college-going patterns of high school graduates in Church of God congregations. (See Chapter 13, point 12). Called for an ongoing process of gathering and having professionally analyzed the annual audits of the colleges, in part to identify trends of concern to allow early and constructive action. Hosted a dinner and program for pastors and senior youth leaders in the St. Louis area (place of this commission meeting) to increase awareness and support of Christian higher education. Commissioned a study of issues related to minority student enrollment in Church of God colleges.

Table 14
Head Count Student Enrollments

The first figure is the total head count of student enrollment each fall semester or quarter, of the colleges predominantly governed by the Church of God. The figure in parentheses is the *percentage* of the first figure represented by *full-time* students.

	1983	1984	1985	1986	1987
Anderson:					
College	1881(92)	1835(91)	1794(91)	1763(92)	1866(89)
Seminary	189(45)	187(36)	176(38)	158(46)	132(48)
Bay Ridge	33(94)	28(61)	38(84)	52(83)	42(95)
Gardner	52(73)	46(76)	45(69)	50(58)	38(82)
Mid-America	332(73)	290(79)	248(79)	231(81)	272(82)
Warner Pacific	425(82)	412(83)	412(79)	390(83)	402(84)
Warner Southern	295(91)	337(83)	294(81)	294(83)	339(79)

Table 15
First-time Church of God Freshmen in Colleges Predominantly Governed by the Church of God

The colleges of the Church of God serve many persons not affiliated with the Church of God. These colleges, nonetheless, value their relationships to this particular constituency and make special efforts to serve its educational needs. One way to observe the level of activity between these colleges and the Church of God is to review the number of freshmen each year who identified themselves as "Church of God" persons.

Colleges Years	AU	BR	GB	MA	WP	WS	TOTAL
1970-71	308	6	19	73	75	25	506
1971-72	276	14	16	70	59	47	482
1972-73	262	19	12	79	58	55	485
1973-74	268	13	13	67	52	60	473
1974-75	288	18	15	73	77	53	524
1975-76	276	7	5	86	53	62	489
1976-77	288	13	22	77	71	71	542
1977-78	257	11	30	75	65	61	499
1978-79	265	17	22	82	63	68	517
1979-80	271	19	18	90	60	64	522
1980-81	281	20	16	69	40	77	503
1981-82	268	8	21	62	40	79	478
1982-83	248	12	29	82	34	69	474
1983-84	271	13	27	57	29	62	459
1984-85	210	8	20	49	30	72	389
1985-86	233	14	12	90	16	50	415
1986-87	217	14	13	64	45	44	397
1987-88	193	9	11	66	17	49	345

AU—Anderson University (undergraduate college only)
BR—Bay Ridge Christian College
GB—Gardner Bible College   WP—Warner Pacific College
MA—Mid-America Bible College WS—Warner Southern College

A graphic view of the distribution of the Church of God freshmen in 1987 follows.

Fall Term, 1987-1988

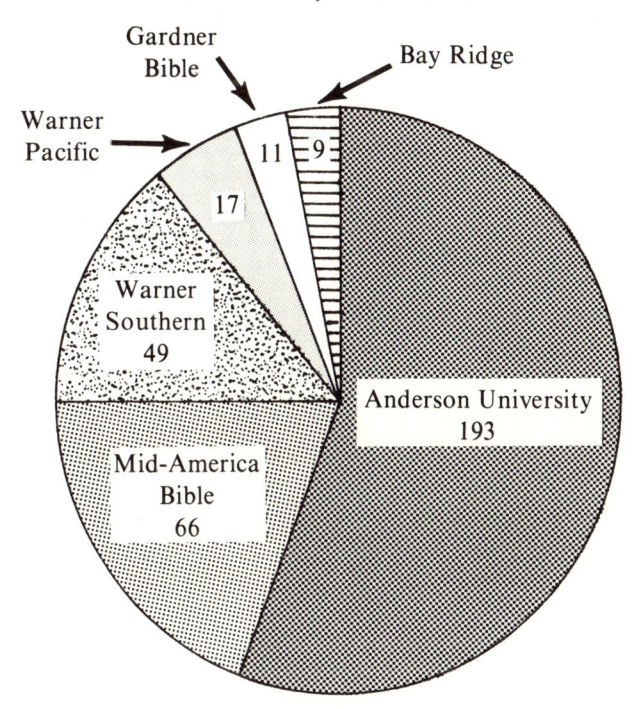

- Gardner Bible: 11
- Bay Ridge: 9
- Warner Pacific: 17
- Warner Southern: 49
- Mid-America Bible: 66
- Anderson University: 193

Church of God Freshmen
Institutions Governed Predominantly
by the Church of God

Table 16
Study of Degree Graduates

The following records the numbers of graduates of formal degree programs offered by the colleges and seminary predominantly governed by the Church of God in the United States and Canada.

	1983	1984	1985	1986	1987
Anderson University (Undergraduate College)					
B.A.	291	258	292	312	351
B.S.N.	0	0	4	6	3
A.A.	26	20	26	21	20
A.S.	52	51	40	54	39
Anderson University (School of Theology)					
M.Div.	27	23	29	31	19
M.R.E.	1	6	3	1	2
M.A.Rel.	9	13	11	17	14
M.Min.	0	0	1	0	0
Bay Ridge Christian College					
B.Rel.	3	2	1	2	2
Gardner Bible College					
B.Th.	5	3	1	2	2
Mid-America Bible College					
B.A.	21	22	20	5	15
B.S.	23	36	49	21	25
A.A.	9	14	19	2	13
Warner Pacific College					
M.R.	4	4	2	2	3
B.A.	40	26	21	30	18
B.S.	44	39	48	53	53
A.A.	2	4	2	1	1
A.S.	0	2	3	1	2
Warner Southern College					
B.A.	54	54	53	53	50
A.A.	10	10	16	11	11
Totals:	621	587	641	625	643
Grand Total in five years:					3,117

Table 17
Church Support for Higher Education

Three questions are answered below: (1) What percentage of the prorated basic budget of the Church of God's Division of World Service has been allocated to higher education? (2) What percentage of that budget was allocated to each institution? (3) What percentage of each institution's operating budget (without auxiliary enterprises) was represented by that World Service allocation? (Note: 1980, for example, means the 1980-1981 church and school year.)

	AU	MA	SOT	STU	WPC	Total
1980 A.	8.52	3.49	5.79	2.69	5.50	25.99
B.	5.00	10.61	48.53		9.69	
1981 A.	8.43	3.61	5.75	2.47	5.46	25.72
B.	5.02	13.23	47.85		8.76	
1982 A.	8.43	3.61	5.75	2.47	5.46	25.72
B.	4.62	11.31	44.19		8.39	
1983 A.	8.35	3.75	5.72	2.38	5.64	25.84
B.	4.55	12.65	46.14		8.77	
1984 A.	8.31	4.00	5.68	2.29	5.57	25.85
B.	4.42	14.54	44.91		8.18	
1985 A.	8.22	4.02	5.60	2.22	5.51	25.57
B.	4.03	14.37	43.16		7.42	
1986 A.	8.14	4.02	5.53	2.17	5.48	25.34
B.	4.17	12.54	40.99		7.66	
1987 A.	8.12	4.10	5.51	2.13	5.48	25.34
B.	3.98	12.81	40.62		7.98	

Legend:
A. Percent of the prorated basic budget allocated by World Service.
B. Percent of operating budget (without auxiliary enterprises) represented by the institution's World Service basic budget allocation.

AU - Anderson University (college only)
MA - Mid-America Bible College
SOT - Anderson University School of Theology
STU - Seminary Tuition Fund
WPC - Warner Pacific College
Total - Total percent of World Service prorated basic budget allocated to higher education

Table 18
World Service Support Per Enrolled Student

The initial general church educational fund established by the General Ministerial Assembly in 1918 was distributed "to the existing Bible training schools in proportion to the number of enrolled students." In more recent years the successor to that fund has been providing substantial financial support, but not to all schools now existing and clearly not in proportion to the number of enrolled students. The funding has been distributed as follows. The receiving institutions are Anderson University, Mid-America Bible College, and Warner Pacific College.

		AU (College)	AU (Seminary)	MA	WPC
1986-87	A.	492,000	334,000	243,000	331,000
	B.	1,763	158	231	390
	C.	279	2,114	1,052	849
1987-88	A.	511,000	347,000	258,000	345,000
	B.	1,866	132	272	402
	C.	274	2,629	949	858

A. Dollars allocated, prorated basic budget, Division of World Service.
B. Head count enrollment, fall semester.
C. Dollars per enrolled student allocated in the prorated basic budget, Division of World Service.

Chapter 13
General Observations and Concerns

The following are general observations, concerns, and projections which arise from a review of the whole history of higher education in the Church of God. They deserve careful reflection by persons wishing to learn from the past so that informed and thoughtful decisions can be made about the future. Information appearing in the text and tables of this volume provide details which illustrate several of the reflections and projections noted below.

1. Low Priority on an Education Establishment.

The time of the beginning of the Church of God movement provided a negative atmosphere in which to evolve movement-related institutions of higher education. In the late nineteenth and early twentieth centuries, orthodox Christianity and the emerging trends in American higher education were increasingly in conflict. The Church of God, if not anti-intellectual in its attitudes, at least tended to put priorities elsewhere.

Given the "liberal" colleges and seminaries its early leaders knew something about, the movement usually was suspicious of scholars probing difficult faith-related questions and openly testing ideas previously unacceptable within the thinking of the movement or even within orthodox Christianity in general. Such probing and testing did not seem the place to put precious energy and time.

Colleges and seminaries typically were associated with the evils of denominationalism. They often were judged to be hotbeds of heresy. While creativity was common within the movement and several prominent persons pursued active intellectual lives, institutions of higher education were not to begin appearing within the movement for several decades. They had low priority on the agendas of "flying" ministers who tended to be suspicious of church-related institutionalism in general.

2. Oriented Around Spiritual Experience.

Compounding the negative institutional atmosphere noted above was the Church of God movement's general approach to Christian theology and discipleship. It was much more experience oriented than it was creedal or propositional. This characteristic typically fostered a repudiation of education as a means to salvation and a distrust of education even as the best way to go about the discovery of truth.

The most important truth was theological in nature, and that truth was best attained in the joining of divine revelation and spiritual discernment. Through the inspired text of the Bible, the Spirit of God would lead an obedient believer into the light of truth. Therefore, understandably, formal education often has not been given high priority in the life of the Church of God and, when it did become prominent, its nature and goals were influenced significantly by this general orientation.

3. Continuing Openness to New Truth.

Countering this tendency to devalue institutions of formal education has been a central conviction about the necessary openness to the guidance of the Holy Spirit. It has been believed consistently within the Church of God movement that God has and is continuing to reveal knowledge about himself and that no person or denomination has arrived at a full understanding of that knowledge. Creeds, then, have been viewed as formalized and necessarily flawed articulations of divine truth. These creeds too easily limit the need for continuing quest and provide a convenient tool for dividing groups of Christians from each other.

Over the decades of the history of the Church of God, therefore, there has been an emphasis on the importance of questing after and discovering truth. This has contributed to a diminishing of the earlier assumption held by many church leaders that persons who increase in knowledge can be expected also to decrease in spirituality. The colleges and seminary of the Church of God have been accepted increasingly as appropriate centers of learning, research, and renewal in the church. But the hesitancy and sometimes even the suspicion remain.

4. Forces of Group Conservatism.

This spirit of genuine openness to learning and growth has struggled to exist in more than theory. There have been in the Church of God, despite its noncreedalism, prominent and influential ministers, "standard" literature, and controlling group perspectives on many subjects. These have provided both group identity and cohesion and a conservative force which on occasion have resisted free exploration and individual thought. There has been a tension between an honestly proclaimed openness to all truth and the controlling influence of the consensus view on a given issue prevailing at any given time. There has been the establishment or threatened establishment of colleges that would be more loyal than the others to the truth which was seen as foundational to the life of the Church of God movement.

Despite the stress on Christian unity and a "movement" identity, such "sectarian" impulses have been felt rather often. These sometimes have sought to clarify the movement's identity and distinctive teachings by embodying themselves in the life of a college (usually a "training" center at first). This has provided some tension, not always unhealthy, with the impulse toward openness and innovation.

5. How "Church of God" Should They Be?

Once institutions of higher education did develop, there was a pattern of concern from the beginning about how to control them. While openness to truth was always deemed a virtue, the more dominant mandate usually felt in the church was to champion the biblical truths perceived in a distinctive way by the Church of God. To preach and train in the known truths was central. There was a very special heritage which any and all educational institutions were expected to herald.

But, particularly as certain of the colleges became strong and attracted constituencies beyond the Church of God, some important questions began to come into focus. How "Church of God" should a Church of God college or seminary be? Is it appropriate for faculty members, administrators, trustees, or a significant percentage of the student body not to be associated directly with the Church of God? How wide a range of theological belief and lifestyle should be permitted? Without question part of the impetus for founding and maintaining the Church of God institutions of higher education was to enable persons to learn and grow and make vital decisions under the movement's influence and with direct exposure to its teachings. But realities of the educational community, the consumer-oriented student marketplace, and the lack of qualified faculty members often have been in tension with this impetus.

What about a merger arrangement such as that of Arlington with Azusa or close ties such as that of Gardner with Camrose Lutheran? What percentage of a faculty, student body, or board of trustees must be "Church of God?" Should the Commission on Christian Higher Education ever be given any real power over the colleges? How much church control of its colleges is essential and possible? These are central questions which will continue to be addressed.

6. Diversity of Educational Missions and Philosophies.

The missions of the several colleges that have developed are diverse in several ways. While the origins of the diversity were many, each a story in itself, eventually there was a tendency to see richness in the diversity. Individuals with their own personalities and agendas have added to the diversity. So have regional needs and special opportunities that have appeared in different settings.

The issues contributing to the diversity included whether a college should go beyond the original task of training church leaders for church vocations, whether "training" and "educating" were the same or different goals, and whether the "liberal arts" was something to be sought or shunned in curricular design. The diversity is very real and quite understandable given the variety of needs to be served and the personalities involved. Healthy forms of institutional competition surely are appropriate and can be constructive, although this has not always been the case among the colleges of the church.

7. Lack of an Educational System.

The approach to organizational matters in the Church of God has had a dramatic impact on the development and inter-relatedness of all of its institutions, including its colleges. The emphasis on local autonomy and the bias against the controlling ability of central organizations or persons has meant that colleges have had maverick-like beginnings, often have been the lengthened shadows of one man or regional agenda, and have benefited from very little effective coordination of their efforts or the available resources. While the Commission on Christian Higher Education has sought some modest role in this area, what typically has prevailed has been the impact of charismatic persons and regional or other special interests. The result has been a general lack of effective coordination, let alone direct control.

This lack of coordination has been judged by some as a strength inherent in a free and creative fellowship and by others as a weakness that has spawned unhealthy competition and a poor stewardship of scarce resources. However it is judged, it is what one would have expected. It is a reflection of the church movement itself as it has struggled to evolve necessary and effective institutions in all areas of its life and mission without such institutions coming to duplicate the "man-rule" evils decried in denominationalism. It also is a central challenge for the future. As Edward L. Foggs put it in his 1988 report to the commission:

> . . . our church colleges must be clear about their mission and their relationship to the church. . . . It calls for a covenant relationship between our colleges and the church setting forth mutual expectations and commitments. The impact of all other trends will, in some measure, be mitigated by the extent to which we embrace this trend and allow it to become mutually operative.

8. Influence of Time and Place.

Colleges associated with the Church of God obviously have been impacted greatly by the particular times and places of their foundings. The manner of their origins and the lack of general church control of their lives certainly contributed to their adaptability and vulnerability to localized circumstances.

The impact of the Great Depression on Warner Memorial University, the volatile influence of the civil rights scene in Mississippi on Bay Ridge Christian College, the favorable results of the central location of Anderson University within the distribution of Church of God people, and the problems caused by the geography and politics of the islands of the West Indies on the Caribbean colleges are clear examples of the influence of time and place. Less obvious but no less influential might be the subtle pressures of American culture, educational organizations, and accrediting associations which have influenced college programs toward equipping students to be "successful" in professional and "materialistic" terms or at least in terms standardized outside these colleges and the Church of God. No church or college lives in a vacuum and the histories of these colleges provide dramatic examples of this truth.

9. Leadership for the Church.

The colleges which have developed in the life of the Church of God have functioned with great influence on the life of the church. They often have been the centers for leadership development, major expenditures of dollar resources, alterations in traditional beliefs and attitudes, creation of new skills and information, and the occasional focal points of sharp controversy.

Anderson University in particular has played a dominant role in all of these regards. It has been the colleges and seminary, predominantly Anderson University, which have led the way in minimizing the intellectual and relational isolation characteristic of the Church of God movement in its earliest years. They have had a broadening effect which, in the main, has brought increasing maturity to the movement. They also at times have raised the question of who should have priority in church authority, the pastor or the professor. This question has found no final answer.

Probably it will not and should not since there is creativity and corrective existing in the ongoing tension between the two.

10. Inadequate Funding Levels.

Adequate funding for higher education in the Church of God always has been a major problem. Some colleges have not survived. Some have been taken into the official family of national agencies, thereby sharing in revenues collected from the general church and distributed by formula.[1] In more recent years the colleges, primarily through state and federal student aid programs, have developed an unwanted but very real reliance on such indirect assistance. A concern is the current trend for the federal government to reduce the money it has been pouring into college student aid. Since Church of God colleges have very small endowments, the loss of such external assistance to their students, whose tuition dollars represent a high percentage of total institutional incomes, is critical.

That loss cannot be expected to be recovered by any major increases in church funding through allocations from the national World Service budget. Such allocations have been significant in the past, particularly when compared with the level at which other church bodies have supported their institutions of higher education. But giving levels in the Church of God have not been increasing rapidly, other national ministries also are in great need of increased funding, and not all of the colleges benefit directly from this national budget. Additional sources of endowment and current giving for operational purposes must be found. New constituencies outside the Church of God must and are being identified to speak to the enrollment problems faced by these colleges.

11. Possible Loss of Institutional Autonomy.

The concern for loss of institutional autonomy has appeared on the legal and accreditation fronts. Many of the laws of the United States as interpreted by courts have placed an increasing number of restrictions even on private, church-related colleges. In addition, Church of God colleges have sought regional and specialized accreditations. The resources expended in this process and the resulting influence on the colleges as they have met standards established externally have been substantial. Presumably such influence in the main has been wholesome and in the direction of educational quality; but without doubt some directions have been forced that otherwise would have been judged of low priority or not desirable at all.

Beyond the legal and accreditation fronts, student enrollment patterns, following national trends, have sifted toward increased numbers of part-time and older, nontraditional students. This shift has increased the diversity of student interests, needs, church affiliations, and often life-styles, lessening their tolerance for campus regulations designed for younger, full-time Christian, residential students. There has even developed a certain sense of being engulfed in a tide of student consumerism when the dollars of such students are needed to enable institutional survival. It has not been and will not be easy to maintain institutional autonomy and integrity in the midst of all these conflicting forces.

12. Decrease of Constituency Loyalty.

Vital to the well-being of church-related colleges is the degree to which they are valued and supported by their own constituencies. Colleges in the Church of God typically have been relatively small and of recent origin. Thus they have not been able to build large, loyal alumni bodies or numbers of affluent friends. Although the colleges have joined the camp meetings in being major centers of cohesion for the Church of God, commitment to these colleges appears to be lessening in recent years. Church of God young persons, not traditionally a strong college-going group in the first place, have been showing less commitment to Church of God institutions just because they are "our colleges." Rather, they have been influenced greatly by the availability, quality, and prestige of particular programs and the problem of the high costs of private higher education as compared to a state institution nearer home.

The Commission on Christian Higher Education conducted parallel studies in 1969 and 1979 to determine the college-going patterns of Church of God young persons. It learned in each instance that about fifty-three percent of the church's high school graduates went immediately on to college and that only twenty-five percent of those going to college chose a Church of God institution. A similar study is being conducted in 1988 to check a fear that this situation has weakened further. The fear is fueled by the knowledge that fewer Church of God freshmen have entered the church's colleges in recent years (an average of 504 per year during the 1970s versus an average of 387 for 1984-1987, a thirty percent reduction!). These circumstances give urgency to the long-standing concern of the commission that somehow families in the church be sensitized to the inherent value of Christian higher education, value worth the extra money required. They also raise the questions of whether and how the church should identify and serve the largest percentage of its college-going young people, most of whom are studying in state sponsored institutions.

13. God Has Been at Work!

The Church of God movement always has been committed more to the work of God itself than to any particular church-related institutions set up to try to get that work done. This obviously has not always made for the strongest institutions within the movement, but it has kept an important perspective before all institutions that have come along. Eventually the movement learned that God works through institutions as well as through gifted individuals. Strong institutions can provide a means for effective, cooperative ministry as well as create the danger of centralized control of aspects of church life. The colleges and seminary that have developed over the years certainly have not been all that God might have wanted. They often have been fragile organizations guided by very human beings in less than ideal circumstances. Nonetheless, *God obviously has been at work!* He has used what has been imperfect, honored the dedication of his gifted servants, and added to his kingdom.

Higher education in the Church of God has taught and learned from students, led and followed the church, profited from and been a friend to various constituencies outside the campus and church communities. The alumni of these Church of God institutions now number in the tens of thousands. They have been prepared to serve—and the scope and magnitude of that service is well worth all the investment that has been made! The Church of God, which has made much of that investment, has, in the process, wrestled much with its own most fundamental premises. As church historian John W. V. Smith has summarized:

> Believing as strongly as they did in divinely called and Holy Spirit-directed leadership, the [Church of God] pioneers rejected all human efforts to "produce" leaders in the church. Yet they quickly learned that the skills of leadership did not necessarily come in the same package with a divine "call." The pilgrimage through the apprentice method, the missionary homes, the training schools, the Bible colleges, the liberal arts colleges, and later a graduate seminary, represents a long struggle with the question of how to provide for leadership that is both divinely empowered and humanly efficient.[2]

14. Hope for the Future.

Since the early 1970s, perceptions of the prospects for American higher education have been influenced strongly by gloomy economic and demographic forecasts of the future. In general, however, the resulting reality has proven more favorable than the forecasts. Higher education has been tenacious and found ways to adjust to the circumstances.

Church-related higher education has seemed particularly vulnerable for the various reasons listed above. But it also has sought available means to face the negative circumstances. It has been forced to clarify its nature and justify its particular mission. It has had to improve its programs of planning and become aggressive in institutional development, particularly the seeking of endowment dollars. It has had to become more conscious of the needs of its immediate constituents. It has become more accountable both to sponsoring churches and to the many organizations and individuals with whom it relates. And it has dedicated itself anew to the concept of service. Finally, it has banded together as never before, with the three liberal arts colleges of the Church of God, for instance, becoming active in the national *Christian College Coalition*.

Creativity, courage, and faith appear to be very much alive. Therefore, the future, laden with problems, is by no means without hope! The call is still the same, to prepare persons for service in the light of the work and commission of Jesus Christ.

Notes

[1] In 1948 the institutions received 22.59 percent of the total annual budget of the national church. In the decade of the 1980s, that percentage has been very stable at about 25.75 percent. See Table 16.

[2] John W. V. Smith, *The Quest for Holiness and Unity* (Anderson, Ind.: Warner Press, 1980), p. 253.

Appendix A
Recommended Criteria for the Establishment of Higher Education Institutions

I. Establishment of Need

Before plans for an institution of higher education are initiated, the need for such an institution should be established first. There are recognized procedures for making such a survey and investigation, and these should be followed.

Educational authorities who administer and coordinate church-related colleges are agreed that such church-related institutions should be established on the basis of one for every 100,000 constituents. With Anderson College and Pacific Bible College in the United States, and Alberta Bible Institute in Canada, we already exceed that recommended ratio.

At this point the Commission's study revealed that in the last twenty years three major educational ventures of the Church of God were unable to continue, namely Warner University, Kansas City Bible School, and Winchester Academy. In addition a number of smaller projects had to be discontinued. These ventures have involved not only great financial loss, but the loss of educational and spiritual morale as well. The Commission feels a strong sense of responsibility to urge the Church to exercise extreme caution lest these unhappy experiences be repeated.

II. Make Certain Financial Resources are Sufficient to Meet the Need and to Insure Continuance of Institution

The Commission felt it could not emphasize too strongly the need for financial stability. It was well aware of the fact that it could not rule out the fine sense of dedication that faculty and administrators manifest in starting a new institution, and their readiness to accept low salaries. Even so, there are minimum expenses that must be underwritten, and for which sources of income must be established. The principal items of expense which should be adequately assured are:

1. *Maintenance of faculty.* Whatever the minimum, this financial support is important to the continuance of the institution. Frequent staff changes can be weakening to the morale of an institution.

2. *Library facilities.* Academic standing is dependent upon library resources. Library requirements for accrediment or respectable standing are not set arbitrarily. They are based on the needs of students for source materials in knowing their field of study.

3. *General educational facilities.* These include classrooms, living quarters, food service facilities and other facilities needed on a campus of Christian higher education.

III. Follow the Generally Accepted Educational Policy of the Church of God

The Commission recognized that no official statement of policy had been made, but that the developing program within the Church had established the following general principles:

1. To develop institutions that have as their objective the four-year college course. This would not preclude the possibility of setting up a Junior College, should such a need be established.

2. The work done by the students in such institutions should lead toward a degree, or a diploma, or formal recognition of some kind that work has been done on a college level. This means that the credits earned would be transferable to other institutions of accredited or acceptable standing.

3. To insure (1) and (2) above, an acceptable curriculum should be established, and an adequate administration set up to maintain these standards. Academic deans and registrars are the responsible administrators for maintaining academic standards.

IV. Should Establish Area and General Cooperation

1. Educational institutions which have regional sponsorship should exercise care to work in harmony and cooperation with existing agencies of cooperation, such as the Ministerial Assembly of such regions or areas.

2. Plans for starting a new institution should have the approval of such regional groups. Enthusiastic endorsement of such projects by the ministers involved go a long way toward inspiring confidence on the part of the general church. It is expected that before ministerial groups sponsor or endorse such projects, investigations and surveys as suggested in the first part of this document will have been made, and along with the cooperation of the Commission on Higher Education, the data will be presented to such interested ministerial groups.

3. *New institutions should not be started on a competitive basis.* In seeking to establish itself, a new school should be careful not to reflect on the program of existing institutions of the Church.

4. *Avoid over-optimistic promotion.* It is recognized that all promotion must carry an optimistic note, yet schools should be conscientious not to claim more for themselves than the institution can actually accomplish. Care should be taken to make clear the standing of the school so students will not infer acceptance of credits by other institutions unless such acceptance has been established. The welfare of the student is of primary importance in an educational program, and everything should be done to give him/her confidence in the educational program and in the integrity of the institution.

V. Relationship to Accrediting Associations

In working with accrediting associations or cooperative agencies, it is recommended that we follow a practice consistent with that of the General Agencies of the Church as authorized by the General Ministerial Assembly.

June 1954
Commission of Higher Education

Appendix B
Who's Who in Church of God Higher Education

The history of the Church of God has been influenced greatly by the ministries of prominent and gifted leaders. This has been true partly because of an abundance of such individuals and partly because of the movement's emphases on the significance of divine gifts and the evils of institutionalism in church life. Nowhere has the crucial role played by outstanding personalities been more obvious than in the history of the movement's activity in the arena of higher education.

What follows is the identifying of selected Christian educators through whose gifts and dedication the several institutions of higher education of the Church of God were founded and led in their significant avenues of service. While some of these persons pursued significant ministries in addition to higher education and sometimes in higher education outside the institutions of the Church of God, only those roles associated with higher education in the Church of God have been noted here. Earned and honorary degrees received have been identified for each person as information was available. Dissertation and book titles have been included when their subject matter related directly to Church of God higher education.

Under God and with his help these persons have made a real difference! Many generations of young persons have learned and grown because of their gifts and dedication to the high calling of God.

BAILEY, Ernest O. (1895-1951)
Dean and Registrar, Warner Memorial University, 1929-1933.

B.S., University of Minnesota.

BELL, Dewayne B. (1920-   )
President, Arlington College, 1963-1969; Assistant to the President, Azusa Pacific University, 1968-1975 and 1976-1977; Vice-President, APU, 1975-1976.

B.A., Anderson University; L.H.D., Azusa Pacific University.

BELTER, Siegfried (1945-1984)
Faculty member, Gardner Bible College, 1971-1984; Dean, GBC, 1975-1984.

B.Th., Gardner Bible College; B.A., University of Alberta; D.D., Gardner Bible College.

BENGTSON, F. Dale (1934-   )
Faculty member, Anderson University, 1960 to present; Dean, School of Arts, Culture, and Religion, AU, 1983 to present.

B.S., Anderson University; M.Mus., University of Wichita; D.M.A., University of Missouri, Kansas City.

BUEHLER, John A. (1916-1981)
Faculty member, Anderson University, 1947-1962; Dean, Bay Ridge Christian College, 1960-1970.

B.A., University of Pennsylvania; B.Th., Anderson University; Ph.D., Indiana University.

BYRUM, Russell Raymond (1889-1980)
One of the founders and first faculty members of Anderson Bible Training School (now Anderson University) in 1917. Author of the influential book *Christian Theology*. Resigned in 1929 from the faculty because he feared the negative impact on the college and the church of the criticism of some ministers about aspects of his teaching.

D.D., Anderson University.

CALDWELL, Irene Smith (1908-1979)
Faculty member, Warner Memorial University, 1930-1932; faculty member, Warner Pacific College, 1945-1966; faculty member, Anderson University School of Theology, 1966-1973; faculty member, Warner Southern College, 1969, 1973-1979.

B.A., Northwestern State Teachers College, Oklahoma; M.A., University of Olklahoma; B.Th., Anderson University; M.A., Oberlin Theological Seminary; Ph.D., University of Southern California.

CALDWELL, Mack M. (1897-1981)
Dean, Southern Bible Institute, 1925-1927; faculty member, Warner Pacific College, 1944-1964; faculty member, Warner

Southern College, 1969-1970. Played significant role in the establishment of the Commission on Christian Higher Education. Min. Dip., Anderson University; B.A., Whittier College; B.Th., Pacific Bible College; M.Ed., University of Oregon; Ed.D., Oregon State University.

CALLEN, Barry L. (1941-   )

Faculty member, Anderson University, 1966 to present; Director, Center for Pastoral Studies, Anderson University School of Theology, 1972-l974; Acting Dean, AU-SOT, 1973-1974 and 1988-1989; Dean, AU-SOT, 1974-1983; Dean, AU, 1983-1988; Vice President for Academic Affairs, AU, 1983 to present. Editor of the Church of God historical volumes titled *The First Century* in 1979. M.Th. title: "Church of God Reformation Movement (Anderson, Indiana): A Study in Ecumenical Idealism." Ed.D. dissertation title: "Faculty Academic Freedom in Member Institutions of the Christian College Coalition." Compiler and editor of "Voice of the Assembly" (contains General Assembly actions related to higher education), 1985. Author of *Preparing For Service: The History of Higher Education in the Church of God,* 1988.

B.A., Geneva College; M.Div., Anderson University School of Theology; M.Th., Asbury Theological Seminary; D.Rel., Chicago Theological Seminary; Ed.D., Indiana University.

CHAPMAN, Milo L. (1915-   )

Faculty member, Warner Pacific College, 1950-1954; Acting President, WPC, 1954-55; Dean, WPC, 1955-1957; President, WPC, 1957-1962; faculty member, WPC, 1963-1964; faculty member, Arlington College, 1964-1967; faculty member, WPC, 1967-1968; Academic Vice-President, WPC, 1968-1973; faculty member, WPC, 1973-1979; President, WPC, 1979-1981; Provost, WPC, 1974 to present. Chair, Commission on Christian Higher Education, 1972-1978.

B.Th., Anderson University; B.D., Th.D., Pacific School of Religion; L.H.D., Anderson University.

CHRISTENSEN, Marshall K. (1941-   )

Faculty member, Warner Pacific Colllege, 1966-1975; Academic Vice-President, WPC, 1975-1978; President, WPC, 1981 to present.

B.A., Warner Pacific College; M.A., Texas Christian University; Ph.D., University of Oregon.

CONLEY, John W. (1932-)

Member, Governing Board, Mid-America Bible College, 1969-1973; Executive Vice-President, MABC, 1973-1975; President, MABC, 1975 to present. Member, Executive Council, American Association of Bible Colleges, 1984 to present.

B.A., Asbury College; M.Th., St. Thomas University; D.D., Asbury College.

COURTNEY, Donald A. (1929-1986)

Faculty member, Anderson University, 1958-1961; faculty member, Anderson University School of Theology, 1961-1966; Executive Secretary-Treasurer, Board of Christian Education of the Church of God, 1966-1986; member, Commission on Christian Higher Education of the Church of God, 1966-1986, chair, 1985-1986. M.Div. thesis title: "A Study of the Development of the Sunday School in the Church of God." Ph.D. dissertation title: "Some Relationships Between Environmental and Institutional Factors and Observed Differences in Classroom Practices in 36 Protestant Church Schools."

B.S., University of Pittsburgh; M.Div., Anderson University School of Theology; M.Ed., Ph.D., University of Pittsburgh.

CROCKETT, Isom R. (1921-)

Dean, Bay Ridge Christian College, 1959-1960. Member, Governing Board, Anderson University, 1962-1982.

B.S., B.A., Anderson University; M.A., Xavier University of New Orleans.

CUMBERBATCH, Carlton T. (1921-)

President, West Indies Theological College, 1959-1988. Thesis title: "The Role of Leadership Training in the Development of the Church of God in the English-speaking Caribbean."

B.A., Anderson University; M.A Rel., Anderson University School of Theology.

CURTIS, Melva W. (1928-)

Faculty member, Mid-America Bible College, 1982 to present;

Dean, MABC, 1986 to present. Member, Commission on Christian Higher Education of the Church of God, 1986 to present.

B.A., California State University, Fresno; M.A. University of San Francisco; Ed.D. candidate, Oklahoma State University.

DAVIS, David W. (1943-   )
President and Dean, Gardner Bible College, 1974-1975

B.S., University of British Columbia; M.Div., Anderson University School of Theology.

DENNISTON, Charles G. (1939-   )
Faculty member, Bay Ridge Christian College, 1972-1982 and 1987 to present; Dean, BRCC, 1976-1977; President, BRCC, 1982-1987; Director of Development, BRCC, 1987 to present.

A.A., Long Beach Community College; B.Th., Bay Ridge Christian College.

DODGE, Harry L. (1914-   )
Dean, Gardner Bible College, 1953-1957.

B.A., University of Cincinnati; B.D., Oberlin Graduate School of Theology; B.Ed., University of Alberta; M.A., University of Akron.

DOTY, Walter M. (1916-   )
Member, Governing Board, Mid-America Bible College, 1955-1966; Dean, MABC, 1955-1969; faculty member, MABC, 1969-1973; Vice-President for Academic Affairs, MABC, 1973-1981; faculty member and Dean of External Studies, MABC, 1981-1983; Dean, Bay Ridge Christian College, 1987 to present. Ed.D. dissertation title: "Factors Which Influenced the Selection of Academic Deans in Thirty-One Texas Public Junior Colleges."

B.A., Anderson University; B.D., North American Baptist Seminary; M.Ed., Ed.D., University of Houston; L.H.D., Anderson University.

DRAKES, Frank (1937-   )
Dean, West Indies Theological College, 1974-1988.

Dip.Theo., West Indies Theological College; B.A., M.A., University of the West Indies.

ERICKSON, Gerald L. (1915-)
Dean, Mid-America Bible College, 1953-1955.

B.Th., Anderson University.

ERICKSON, Joyce Q. (1939-)
Dean of the faculty, Warner Pacific College, 1983-1987.

B.A., North Central College; M.A., Ph.D., University of Washington.

EUBANKS, Odus K. (1933-)
Faculty member, Mid-America Bible College, 1975-1981; Vice-President for Academic Affairs, MABC, 1981-1985.

B.S., Southeast Missouri State University; M.R.E., Southwestern Baptist Theological Seminary; M.Div., Anderson University School of Theology; Ed.D., Texas Southern University.

FOLTZ, Louis G. (1947-)
Faculty member, Warner Pacific College, 1976-1981 and 1983 to present; Dean, WPC, 1981-1983.

A.A., Napa College; B.A., M.A., Ph.D., University of California, Berkeley.

FULTON, Leroy M. (193-)
Member, Governing Board, Warner Southern College, 1964-1969, chair, 1966-1969; President and faculty member, WSC, 1969 to present.

B.A., Anderson University; M.Div., Anderson University School of Theology; D.D., Anderson University.

GARDNER, Harry C. (1894-1961)
Principal, Gardner Bible College, 1933-1945; President, GBC, 1945-1953, 1957-1961; Dean, GBC, 1933-1950; chair, governing board, GBC, 1933-1950.

B.Th., Anderson University; D.D., American College.

GAULKE, Max R. (1910-)
President, Mid-America Bible College, 1953-1975.

B.A., Anderson University; B.D., Chicago Theological Seminary; M.A., University of Houston; D.D., Anderson University.

GERMANY, James Horace (1914-)
President, Bay Ridge Christian College, 1959-1982, Dean, 1970-1971, 1975-1976.

B.Th., L.H.D., Anderson University.

GILLIAM, E. Joe (1929-)
President, Warner Pacific College, 1966-1979.

L.H.D., Anderson University.

GOODRIDGE, MARTIN (1941-)
President, West Indies Theological College, 1988 to present.

B.A., London Bible College; M.A.Rel., Anderson University School of Theology.

GOUGH, Louis F. (1910-1978)
Faculty member, Warner Pacific College, 1952-1956; faculty member, Anderson University School of Theology, 1956-1960; assistant to the president, WPC, 1960-1962; President, WPC, 1962-1966.

B.Th., B.S., Anderson University; B.D., Duke University; Th.D., Princeton Theological Seminary.

GRAY, Albert F. (1886-1969)
Faculty member, Anderson University, 1929-1930; President, Warner Pacific College, 1937-1957; faculty member, WPC, 1957-1960, 1963-1969; chair, governing board, AU, 1931-1948.

D.D., Anderson University.

GRUBBS, Jerry C. (1940-)
Member, governing board, Warner Southern College, 1972-1974; faculty member, Anderson University School of Theology, 1973-1988; Director, Center for Pastoral Studies, AU-SOT, 1980-1984; Dean, AU-SOT, 1983-1988; Vice-President for Student Life and Human Resources, AU, 1988 to present. Ed.D. dissertation title: "A Study of Faculty Members and Students in Selected Mid-Western Schools of Theology to Determine Whether Their Education Orientation is Andragogical or Pedagogical."

B.A., Northeast Louisiana University; M.R.E., Anderson University School of Theology; M.S., Ed.D., Indiana University.

HASTINGS, Raymond E. (1917-)
Faculty member, Mid-America Bible College, 1965-1970, Dean of Students, MABC, 1965-1967; faculty member and Dean, Bay Ridge Christian College, 1971-1974.

B.A., Anderson University; M.Div., Anderson University School of Theology.

HAZEN, Robert (1923-)
President, Gardner Bible College, 1977 to present.

B.Th., Anderson University; D.D., Warner Pacific College.

HOWARD, John Alan (1949-)
Faculty member, Gardner Bible College, 1982 to present; Dean, GBC, 1984 to present.

B.A., Anderson University; M.R.E., M.Div., Anderson University School of Theology; S.T.M., University of Winnipeg.

JACK, Ronald M. (1934-)
Faculty member, Anderson University, 1958-1959, 1971; faculty member, Warner Southern College, 1974 to present; Vice-President for Academic Affairs, WSC, 1983 to present.

B.A., Anderson University; M.Div., Anderson University School of Theology; M.S., Ph.D., Purdue University.

JANUTOLO, D. Blake (1952-)
Faculty member, Anderson University, 1977 to present; Dean, School of Theoretical and Applied Science, AU, 1985 to present.

B.S., West Virginia University; Ph.D., Virginia Polytechnic Institute and State University.

JOINER, C. Herbert, Jr. (1918-1974)
President, Arlington College, 1954-1960.

B.A., Anderson University; M.Div., Louisville Presbyterian Seminary.

JONES, Kenneth E. (1920-)
Dean, Gardner Bible College, 1950-1951; member, governing board, Jamaica School of Theology, 1960; Principal and faculty member, Jamaica School of Theology, 1962; faculty member, Mid-America Bible College, 1963-1965; member, Commission on Christian Higher Education, 1963-1965, 1985-1986; faculty

member, Warner Pacific College, 1965-1974; faculty member, MABC, 1974-1987; Dean, MABC, 1985-1986.

B. Th., Anderson University; B.D., Oberlin Graduate School of Theology; M.Th., Winona Lake School of Theology; Ph.D., International Institute for Advanced Studies; D.D., Warner Pacific College.

KEMPIN, Albert J. (1900-   )
Dean, Arlington College, 1954-1956.

B.A., Taylor University; M.Th., University of Southern California; Ph. D., Los Angeles Baptist Theological Seminary.

LINDEMUTH, Marvin H. (1923-   )
Acting Dean, Warner Pacific College, 1963-1964; Dean, WPC, 1964-1968; faculty member, Anderson University, 1968-1988; assistant to the dean, AU, 1968-1971.

B.S., Seattle Pacific University; M.Ed., University of Washington; Ph.D., University of Michigan.

LINN, Otto F. (1887-1965)
Faculty member, Anderson University, 1932-1937; Dean, Warner Pacific College, 1942-1955.

B.A., B.S., M.A., Phillips University; Ph.D., Divinity School, University of Chicago.

LOEWEN, Curtis E. (1927-   )
Dean, Warner Pacific College, 1973-1975.

B.S., Ed.M., Ed.D., Oregon State University.

MACHOLTZ, James D. (1926-1985)
Faculty member, Anderson University, 1953-1985; Dean, School of Theoretical and Applied Science, AU, 1983-1985.

B.S., Anderson University, M.S., University of Michigan; M.S., P. E. D., Indiana University.

MARTIN, Earl Leslie (1892-1961)
Faculty member, Anderson University, 1930-1950; Dean, Anderson University School of Theology, 1950-1953; faculty member, Anderson University, 1953-1957; vice-chair, Commission on Christian Higher Education, 1958; visiting professor, West Indies Theological College, 1958; Acting President, Arlington College, 1960-1961.

B. Th., Anderson University; M.A., Northwestern University; B.D., D.D., Anderson University.

MASSEY, James Earl (1930-   )

Principal, Jamaica School of Theology, 1963-1966; faculty member and campus pastor, Anderson University, 1969-1977; chair, Commission on Christian Higher Education, 1969-1971 and member, 1987 to present; faculty member, Anderson University School of Theology, 1981-1984.

B.R.E., B.Th., Detroit Bible College; M.A., Oberlin Graduate School of Theology; D.D., Asbury Theological Seminary.

MILLER, Adam W. (1896-   )

Faculty member, Anderson University, 1941-1962; chair, Study Committee on Graduate Ministerial Training (led to establishment of Anderson University School of Theology); Dean, AUSOT, 1953-1962.

B.A., Anderson University; M.A., Butler University; D.D., Anderson University.

MILLER, E. Darlene (1940-   )

Faculty member, Anderson University, 1965 to present; Dean, School of Social and Professional Studies, AU, 1983 to present.

B.S., Anderson University; M.A., Ed.D., Ball State University.

MILLER, Gene (1929-   )

Faculty member, Mid-America Bible College, 1968-1985; Acting Dean, MABC, 1969-1970; faculty member, Anderson University School of Theology, 1985 to present.

B.A., Anderson University; M.Div., Anderson University School of Theology; Ph.D., Duke University.

MILLER, T. Franklin (1910-   )

Executive Secretary, National Board of Christian Education, 1945-1966; vice-chair, Commission on Christian Higher Education, 1965-1966; faculty member, Anderson University School of Theology, 1950, 1975-1980; Director, Center for Pastoral Studies, 1976-1980.

B.A., Gordon College of Theology and Missions; B.D., Butler University School of Religion; D.D., Anderson University.

MORRISON, John Arch (1893-1965)
Faculty member and Assistant Principal, Anderson University, 1919-1923; Principal, AU, 1923-1925; President, AU, 1925-1958; member, governing board, AU, 1925-1954.

D.D., Anderson University.

NEWBERRY, Gene W. (1915-   )
Faculty member, Anderson University, 1946-1950; faculty member, Anderson University School of Theology, 1950-1980; Dean, AU-SOT, 1962-1974.

B.A., Denison Unversity; B.Th., Anderson University; Ph.D., Duke University; D.D., Rio Grande College.

NICHOLSON, Robert A. (1923-   )
Faculty member, Anderson University, 1945 to present; Dean, AU, 1958-1983, Vice-President for Academic Affairs and Dean, AU, 1971-1983; President and member, governing board, AU, 1983 to present; member, Commission on Christian Higher Education, 1958 to present, chair, 1963-1968 and 1983-1984, vice-chair, 1959-1962 and 1969-1983.

B.S., Anderson University; M.A., Ph.D., New York University.

OLT, George Russell (1895-1958)
Faculty member and Dean, Anderson University, 1925-1958; member, governing board, AU, 1925-1945

B.Ph., B.A., Lebanon University; B.A., Wilmington College; M.A., University of Cincinnati; L.H.D., Anderson University.

PAPPAS, Thomas Nicholas (1936-   )
Faculty member, Anderson University, 1962-1976; faculty member, Warner Pacific College, 1976-1978; Dean, WPC, 1978-1981.

B.A., M.A., Wayne State University; Ph.D., Michigan State University.

RAMSEY, George H. (1922-   )
Faculty member, Anderson University, 1947-1948; faculty member and President, Arlington College, 1961-1963; faculty member, AU, 1963-1984.

B.S., Anderson University; B.D., Princeton Theological Seminary.

RATZLAFF, Leslie W. (1915-   )
Faculty member, Warner Pacific College, 1956-1963; Dean, WPC, 1958-1963; administrator in advance of the beginning of Warner Southern College, 1966-1968; President, Warner Southern College, 1968-1969; Dean, WSC, 1968-1983. Ed.D. dissertation title: "The Implementation of Christian Goals in Christian Liberal Arts Colleges."

B.A., B.Th., Anderson University; M.Div., Princeton Theological Seminary; M.A., Ed.D., Teachers College and Union Theological Seminary, Columbia University; L.H.D., Anderson University.

REARDON, Robert H. (1919-   )
Assistant to the the President, Anderson University, 1947-1952; Executive Vice-President, AU, 1952-1958, President, AU, 1958-1983. B.D. thesis titled: "The Doctrine of the Church and the Christian Life in the Church of God Reformation Movement." Author, *The Early Morning Light* (reflections on the first fifty years of the Church of God movement), 1979.

B.A., Anderson University; B.D., Oberlin Graduate School of Theology; D.Min., Vanderbilt University; L.H.D., DePauw University; L.H.D., Anderson University.

RIGEL, W. Malcolm (1926-   )
Member, governing board, Warner Southern College, 1964-1968; faculty member, Dean of Students, WSC, 1968-1979; associate faculty member, Anderson University School of Theology, 1979-1983; faculty member, WSC, 1983-1987.

A.A., Vincennes University; B.A., Anderson University; M.A., University of South Florida; S.T.M., University of Dubuque Theological Seminary; S.T.D., Emory University.

SAGO, Paul E. (1931-   )
Vice-President for Financial Affairs, Anderson University, 1968-1976; President, Azusa Pacific University, 1976 to present. Ph.D. dissertation title: "Faculty and Administrative Concepts Relating to Shared Authority in Financial Decision-Making."

B.S., Findlay College; M.S., St. Francis College; Ph.D., Walden University.

SARJU, Sawak (1938-   )
Dean, Bay Ridge Christian College, 1974-1975.

Diploma, West Indies Theological College; B.A., Pacific College; M.R.E., Mennonite Biblical Seminary; D.D., American Bible Institute.

SCHIECK, Gordon A. (1914-   )
Dean, Gardner Bible College, 1951-1953; Acting President., GBC, 1953-1955; President, GBC, 1967-1974; Interim President, GBC, 1975-1977.

B.A., Anderson University; M.A., Syracuse University.

SHACKLETON, Frederick G. (1922-   )
Faculty member, Anderson University, 1946-1950; faculty member, Warner Pacific College, 1950-1954; faculty member, Arlington College, 1954-1956; Dean, Arlington College, 1956-1968; faculty member, Azusa Pacific University, 1968 to present.

B.A., Macalester College; M.A., Butler University; D.D., Western Evangelical Seminary.

SMITH, Donald E. (1935-   )
Faculty member, Mid-America Bible College, 1970-1973; Dean, MABC, 1970-1973.

B.S., M.Ed., University of Illinois; Ed.D., Illinois State University.

SMITH, John W.V. (1914-1984)
Faculty member, Warner Pacific College, 1949-1952; faculty member, Anderson University School of Theology, 1952-1980, Associate Dean, AU-SOT, 1968-1983; visiting professor, Warner Southern College, 1969. Historian of the Church of God, 1957-1984, authoring in 1980 the comprehensive history of the Church of God titled *The Quest for Holiness and Unity*. Visiting professor, international Bible schools of the Church of God, 1983-1984. Ph.D. dissertation title: "The Approach of the Church of God (Anderson, Indiana) and Comparable Groups to the Problem of Christian Unity."

B.A., Northwestern Oklahoma State College; M.A., University of Oklahoma; Ph.D., University of Southern California.

STAFFORD, Gilbert W. (1938-)
Faculty member, Anderson University School of Theology, 1976 to present; Associate Dean, AU-SOT, 1980 to present. Th.D. dissertation titled: "Experiential Salvation and Christian Unity in the Thought of Seven Theologians of the Church of God (Anderson, Indiana).

B.A., Anderson University; M.Div., Andover Newton Theological School; Th.D., Boston University School of Theology.

WILLIAMS, Elbert (1945-)
Dean, Bay Ridge Christian College, 1977-1987; Executive Vice-President, BRCC, 1983-1987.

B.Th., Bay Ridge Christian College; M.S., Henderson State University.

WILLIAMS, Robert C. (1941-)
President, Bay Ridge Christian College, 1987 to present. Member, Commission on Christian Higher Education of the Church of God, 1984-1987.

B.Th., Bay Ridge Christian College; M.Ed., Ed.D., University of Southern Mississippi.

WILSON, Joseph Turner (1876-1954)
Principal and founder, Anderson Bible Training School (now Anderson University), 1917-1923, member, governing board, Anderson University, 1918-1946, chair, 1925-1931; President and founder, Warner Memorial University, 1929-1933.

Graduate, Slippery Rock State Normal School; D.D., Anderson University.

WIUFF, Jarvis C. (1925-)
Dean, Gardner Bible College, 1962-1968.

B.A., Anderson University.

YAMABE, Richard N. (1928-)
Dean, Gardner Bible College, 1957-1962 and 1968-1974.

B.A., University of British Columbia; M.Div., Anderson University School of Theology.

Appendix C
International Institutions Associated with the Church of God

In addition to the institutions of higher education in the United States, Canada and the Caribbean, all detailed elsewhere in this volume, the following are other institutions associated with the Church of God.

AFRICA

Kima Theological College
P. O. Box 75
Maseno, Kenya,
    EAST AFRICA

Shule Ya Biblia
Kanisa la Mungu
S. L. P. 146
Babati, Tanzania,
    EAST AFRICA
James Sharp, Director

ASIA

Asian Bible College
Ecclesia, P. O. Box 2219
Cochin 682 024, SOUTH INDIA
Rev. P. V. Jacob, Director

AUSTRALIA

Sydney Centre for Christian Studies
19 Matthew Avenue
Heckenberg, N. S. W. 2168

MIDDLE EAST

Mediterranean Bible College
P. O. Box 165164
Salam Street, Ashrafieh
Beirut, LEBANON
Dr. Fouad B. Melki, Principal

LATIN AMERICA

La Buena Tierra Peruana
Casilla 161
Pucallpa, PERU

Instituto Teologico Posadas
C. C. 12
3300 Posadas, Misiones,
  ARGENTINA
Victor Ruzak, Director

Centro de Ensenanzas
  Ministeriales
Apartado 6048
San Jose 1000, COSTA RICA
Keith and Gloria Plank,
  Directors

Instituto Biblico "Boa Terra"
Caixa Postal 2221
80001 Curitiba, PR, BRAZIL
Nelson N. Junges, Director

Instituto Biblico "La Buena Tierra"
Apartado 665
Guatemala City, GUATEMALA, CENTRAL AMERICA
Isai Calderon, Director

Index of Persons

Acheson, Esther, 92
Adams, John, 54
Adams, Juanita and Robert, 100
Adcock, Elver, 107-108
Allen, A. Patrick, 48
Bacani, Rolando, 94
Bailey, Ernest O., 105-107, 109, 200
Bailey, George W., 111
Bailey, Pearl, 104, 106
Baker, Marvin, 175
Barber, Jay, 121
Barnett, Edgar, 105
Barnett, Florence Orr, 128, 133
Barnett, Ross, 70
Batdorf, Dora, 104
Batdorf, John, 104, 107
Bates, Charles, 133
Bauer, Esther, 35
Beach, Verda, 175
Beard, Norman, 40, 49
Bell, Dewayne B., 55, 59-60, 62-63, 200
Belter, Siegfried, 83, 86, 88, 201
Bengtson, F. Dale, 201
Benson, Charles, 59-60, 62
Benson, Joseph, 127
Berquist, Maurice, 52-55, 61-63, 159
Berry, R. L., 32, 156, 160
Blanchard, John, 6
Boone, Daisy Maiden, 37, 113
Boucher, M. B., 109
Boyer, Harold, 134, 136, 165
Bradley, James, 46
Breitweiser, Paul, 105-106
Brooks, H. A., 16, 25

Brooks, Lawrence, 15
Brumfield, Donald, 100
Buck, George, 145
Buehler, John A., 76, 201
Burchett, James, 129
Burgess, O. A., 111
Burns, George W., 67, 69-70
Butler, Lloyd, 93
Byers, Andrew L., 14
Byers, C. E., 33
Byrum, Bessie L., 26
Byrum, Enoch E., 14, 15, 18
Byrum, Russell R., vii, 21, 25-27, 29-30, 32, 59, 63, 65, 201
Caldwell, Irene Smith, 106, 114, 118, 134, 201
Caldwell, Mack M., 63, 65, 67, 157, 159, 161, 164, 168, 201-202
Callen, Barry L., v, 40, 42, 44, 48, 123, 135, 150-151, 175, 202
Campbell, Nettie, 105
Chapman, Milo L., 43, 61-62, 84, 114-116, 118-119, 121, 123-124, 165, 168, 175, 202
Cheeks, Charlie, 67, 127-128, 132-134, 159
Chesterman, Harold, 68, 71
Christensen, Marshall K., 121-122, 124, 202
Chugg, J. Milton, 88
Clark, Robert, 134, 136
Clausen, H. C., 26
Clear, Val, 15, 17, 69, 174
Cleary, Kenneth W., 130-131, 138
Campbell, J. E., 26

Cole, George L., 18
Cole, Jeremiah, 14
Commager, Henry S., 4
Conley, John W., 98-101, 203
Conover, Eugene, 62
Coody, Burt, 128
Coolidge, Ralph, 146, 153
Courtney, Donald A., 128, 175, 203
Crockett, Isom, 66-71, 76, 203
Crockett, Ola, 68
Crose, Kenneth, 106, 118
Crose, Lester, 106, 107
Cumberbatch, Carlton, 146-148, 150, 152-153, 203
Cumberbatch, Edward, 152
Cumberbatch, Theodosia Francis, 147, 153
Curtis, Melva W., 101, 203
Davis, David W., 84-85, 88, 204
Dawson, I. K., 159
Denniston, Charles G., 74, 76, 204
Denton, Mark, 53
Denton, Wilford, 56-57, 59, 62
Dodge, Harry L., 83, 88, 204
Doty, Walter M., 43, 75-76, 94, 97, 100-101, 204
Drakes, Frank, 148, 153, 204
Drakes, Hugh, 153
Durbin, Kathie, 123
Dwight, Timothy, 5
Egtvedt, Evelyn, 120
Eisenhower, Dwight D., 37
Engst, Irene, 87
Erickson, Gerald L., 92-93, 100-101, 204
Erickson, Joyce 122, 124, 205
Ervin, Preston, 76
Eubanks, Odus K., 100-101, 205

Ewert, Irene and Wilhelm, 81
Farmer, Ralph, 84-85
Flint, Oscar J., 30
Finney, Charles, 12
Foggs, Edward L., 189
Foltz, Louis, 124, 205
Ford, Gerald, 120
Forrest, Aubrey, 106, 159
Fowler, Ronald J., 44, 48
Franklin, Lottie, 113
Frederici, Louise, 28
Froese, Walter, 85-87
Fulton, Leroy M., 131-134, 136-138, 205
Gaither, William and Gloria, 45
Gardner, Harry C., 30, 77-80, 82-83, 86, 88, 205
Gaulke, Isabelle, 92
Gaulke, Max R., 89-95, 97, 100-101, 205
Germany, J. Horace, 43, 66-72, 74-76, 205
Gilliam, E. Joe, 118-121, 124, 206
Goodman, Delena, 38
Goodridge, Martin, 153, 206
Gough, Louis F., 58, 69, 114, 116-118, 121, 124, 206
Gray, Albert F., 19, 111-113, 115, 124, 156, 174, 206
Gray, Dorothy, 113
Gray, Harold, 113
Gray, Rosa, 113
Green, Edith, 120
Gross, Ernest, 131, 133
Grubbs, Dwight, 100
Grubbs, J. Perry, 134, 136
Grubbs, Jerry C., 45, 48, 175, 206
Haggard, Cornelius, 59, 63

Hall, Thomas M., 83, 88
Harp, Harry L., 127, 159, 165
Harper, William R., 8
Hartselle, Cecil, 133
Hastings, Elna Mae, 142
Hastings, Raymond E., 76, 142, 206
Hatfield, Mark, 120
Hathcoat, Horace, 158-159
Hazen, Robert, 85-86, 88
Heffren, H. C., 87
Heinly, F. W., 19
Helms, Mabel, 26
Hofstadter, Richard, 5
Howard, John, 83, 86, 88
Hubbard, C. Anderson, 114
Hughes, John Wesley, 84
Irving, Albert, 88
Jack, Ronald M., 134, 138
Jakeway, Wade, 134
Janutolo, D. Blake, 207
Jefferson, Thomas, 4
Johnson, Betty Jo, 148
Johnson, Deryl, 136
Johnson, Donald D., 123, 148, 153
Johnson, Henry, 127
Johnson, O. L., 52
Joiner, C. Herbert, Jr., 51-57, 61, 63, 207
Joiner, Ronald, 164
Jones, Kenneth E., 82, 88, 100-101, 103, 142, 207-208
Kahn, A. D., 112
Kane, John, 39
Kardatzke, Carl, 35, 39, 106, 107
Kardatzke, Elmer, 106
Kardatzke, Lucille, 107
Kempin, Albert J., 53, 63, 208
King, Doug, 54

King, W. W., 142
Kirks, Ruth, 100
Koglin, Anna, 28
Lehmann, Walter, 153
Lewis, Pearl, 113
Lincoln, Abraham, 6
Lindemuth, Marvin, 116, 118-119, 124, 175, 208
Lindgren, Elsie and Victor, 80
Linn, Otto F., vii, 114-115, 124, 158-159, 208
Little, Ralph, 143
Loewen, Curtis, 124, 208
Lopez, Amy, 35
Luther, Martin, 6
Lynch, Leopold, 146
MacDonald, William, 100
McGrath, Earl J., 119-120
Macholtz, James D., 208
Malbone, Thomas, 175
Martin, David, 51-52
Martin, Earl L., 35, 38-39, 48, 57, 63, 149, 175, 208
Marvel, Gerald, 53-54, 57, 62
Massey, James E., 72, 143-145, 175, 209
Menchinger, Fred, 175
Merioles, Felipe, 94
Miller, Adam W., 19, 25-26, 38-39, 42, 48, 161, 165, 209
Miller, E. Darlene, 209
Miller, Gene, 100-101, 209
Miller, Oakley, 147-148
Miller, T. Franklin, 17, 38, 67, 158, 161, 164-165, 168, 175, 209
Monroe, D. S. Warner, 35, 114
Monroe, Sarah, 79
Moore, Ero, 133, 136
Moore, Ronald, 45
Morgan, Fred, 136

Morison, Samuel E., 4
Morrison, John A., 29-34, 36-39, 47-48, 104, 128, 159, 165, 210
Murrell, Felix, 128
Myers, Linfield, 29, 37, 47
Neal, John, 53
Nelms, Daniel, 87
Nelson, Cressie, 105
Nelson, Leona, 66
Neuman, John, 105
Newberry, Gene W., 38-39, 42, 48, 210
Newell, Arlo F., 127
Nicholson, Robert A., 39-40, 43-48, 72, 84, 128, 175, 210
Norholm, Kresten, 94
Olson, George, 142, 144
Olson, Mary, 142
Olson, Nellie, 30, 141-142, 144
Olt, George R., 30-31, 34, 36-39, 48, 83, 114, 127-128, 210
Osnes, Larry, 40
Owens, R. H., 156
Pappas, Thomas N., 124, 210
Patton, Norman and Marge, 55, 62
Payne, Clifford, 147-148, 153
Perry, E. E., 158
Phelps, J. W., 20, 141, 156
Phillips, Harold L., 38
Pickett, Donald, 136
Plough, W. I., 165
Proctor, Earl, 147
Prunty, Kenneth, 52
Pumpelly, Robert J., 100-101
Pye, George, 152
Raines, Carl, 128, 132
Ramsey, Alva, 141
Ramsey, George H., 57-58, 61-63, 210

Ratzlaff, Leslie W., 43, 115, 124, 130-136, 138, 142, 211
Ratzlaff, Nina, 132, 136
Reardon, E. A., 18
Reardon, Jerry Hurst, 35
Reardon, Robert H., vii, 19, 30, 38-41, 43, 47-48, 118, 211
Reed, William E., 68, 159
Rees, Paul S., 120
Reynolds, Harry and Lenora, 105-108
Rice, Herschell, 53, 62, 159
Rice, Hillery, 159
Richardson, O. M., 132
Richardson, Ray, 70-71
Richey, Everett, 57, 60, 62
Rigel, W. Malcolm, 127, 130-133, 136, 211
Riggle, Herbert M., 13
Roark, Warren C., 159
Rohr, Loren, 93
Rouse, Wesley, 136
Rowe, A. T., 47, 67, 159
Rowe, Ida Byrd, 164
Ryan, Alexander, 88
Sago, Paul E., 60-63, 211
Sarju, Sawak, 76, 212
Schieck, Gordon, 52, 82-85, 87-88, 165, 212
Schield, Vern, 36, 147
Schield, Wilbur, 147
Schlatter, Henry, 112
Schmuki, John, 113
Shackleton, Frederick G., 54, 60-63, 168, 212
Sharp, Samuel, 161, 165, 175
Sharpe, Hollie, 72, 175
Shaw, J. Frank, 28
Sherwood, H. A., 26
Shultz, Claire, 146-147, 153
Skaggs, Wilbur, 113

Smith, Beatrice and Louis, 105
Smith, Donald E., 97, 101, 212
Smith, Frederick G., 26-29, 31-34, 174
Smith, Frellsen, 91, 105
Smith, John W. V., 38, 47, 53, 114-115, 123, 149, 159, 164, 194, 212-213
Smith, Richard, 131
Sonnenberg, Gustav, 81-82
Stafford, Gilbert W., 213
Stewart, James, 68-70
Stone, Candace, 37
Strege, Merle D., vii
Strong, Marie, 128
Struthers, Charles and Florence, 142
Studebaker, Eula and Hersel, 132
Sunday, Billy, 8
Swart, Carl, 51
Swinehart, E. V., 112
Tasker, G. P., 112
Teasley, D. O., 16, 112, 156
Thompson, John, 124
Thor, J. C., 175
Tierney, Clifford, 51
Trick, Nelson, 100
Trueblood, D. Elton, 120
Tufts, Gorham, 18
Turnbull, Ralph G., 120
Van Dyke, Jack, 35
Vines, Fred, 127
Wade, James, 165, 175
Ward, Hutchins, 105
Warner, Daniel S., 12-15, 18, 20, 38, 63, 65-66, 115, 154-155
Welch, Douglas, 83
Wellman, Sam, 134
White, Harold, 132
Whitehead, Edward, 124
Wiens, Jacob, 80
Williams, Edgar, 134
Williams, Elbert, 76, 213
Williams, Emery, 67
Williams, Robert C., 74-76, 213
Williamson, Lowell J., 120
Wilson, Charles E., 37
Wilson, Johnny ("Jumpin"), 36
Wilson, Joseph T., 25-27, 29-30, 48, 89, 103-107, 109, 213
Winland, Jack, 54
Wiuff, Jarvis C., 88, 213
Wolfram, E. E., 159
Wolkow, Hugh, 88
Wright, Walker, 79
Yamabe, Richard N., 83, 88, 213
Young, Edith, 141-142